DEPRESSION
LIES

How To Reclaim Your Life and
Make It A Masterpiece

Breakfree Forever Publishing

Dr Francis Ikhenemoh

DEDICATION

I dedicate this book to a man of peace and wisdom, my father Joseph Ikhenemoh and to my dearest mother, Juliana Ikhenemoh, the light of my world.

"And in the end it's not the years in your life that count. It's the life in your years."
— Abraham Lincoln

"Grief is love with no place to go."
— Jamie Anderson

CONTENT

FOREWORD

Being an entrepreneur, business mentor and international speaker and having trained thousands of people all across the world, every now and then someone turns up that catches my eye. The person who caught my eye recently is none other than Dr Francis Ikhenemoh.

Now why did this man catch my eye? Because what I discovered is that this man has a gift. He has a talent, he has a skill, he has a passion, and he has a heart that makes him want to make this world a better place.

Why is that important? Well, you see being an ex-psychiatric nurse myself and being in the medical profession, I understand one thing, and that is when you are in the medical profession it is sometimes possible for us to forget about human beings. What I have discovered about Dr Francis Ikenemoh is this, it's that this man although he is a medical Dr he has one of the biggest hearts ever, and he has a deep, deep, deep interest in working with people and helping them overcome depression. Not in your usual ways of giving medication but by using a very, clever system that he has discovered that revolves around six core things that every person should do. If they literally want to get rid of depression and reclaim their lives they can make it a masterpiece just like he describes.

Why should you listen to him? Because at the end of the day there are probably many people out there who could give you advice, who could tell you what you should and shouldn't be doing, but does everybody know how to really get you unstuck?

Well let me tell you what qualifies him to make you do that:

- He is a medical Doctor
- He is trained in mental health and mental awareness
- He has helped countless people overcome depression, not just through drugs but by talking to them.
- You will also be getting help from somebody who, he himself struggled with depression and has risen above it to become who he is.

So, I highly recommend the journey you are about to embark on reading this book, it will be one that will change your life for good. It might sound cliché when I say 'change your life' because I am sure it is not the first time you will have heard it, but what I want to say is this:

If you are open, willing and ready to take charge of your life and to move forwards with your life, to start living life on your terms again, then pick up this book, read it, follow what he tells you and I promise you, great things will happen for you.

Enjoy the book and be sure to implement everything that he teaches you.

Jessen James
Founder of Global Success
Author of The Great Business Jailbreak

INTRODUCTION

Mental illness is the greatest epidemic happening to humankind for the past forty to fifty years. One in ten people experience a mental health issue and one in four are sure to suffer a depressive episode at some point in their lives. Some of the hallmark symptoms of depression, as defined by the World Health Organisation, include, low mood, indifference, an inability to experience pleasure, feelings of guilt, low self-worth, disturbed sleep patterns, and appetite. Depression affects numerous families, individuals and organisations worldwide and it has become a greater epidemic in the youth of today as they are more widely affected in today's society compared to twenty-five years ago.

This debilitating condition is destroying homes and sometimes going undetected until it is too late and severe damage is already done.

At the moment we are all living in unprecedented times but depression has always existed and, unfortunately, will continue to exist. I have noticed in the Western culture that depression has skyrocketed and is at the point where it has put a strain on our society. The question on the minds of those affected by this illness is 'how do we solve this problem or minimise this epidemic?' There have been many studies and theories about what depression is and the solution, but there has never been one solid answer to this question. For some it's counselling or medication and others nutrition, however, looking at the age we are in where information technology is at its peak and time has revolutionised, the way I see it is that depression lies.

One may be wondering what it is that I am talking about. I am stating the fact that depression is one of the greatest liars to walk on the face of this earth. Depression works very hard to tell us lies and create beliefs of so many things that are not true.

In this book I will be digging deeper into the lies of depression, how it makes you feel, the things it may be causing you to think and believe about yourself and others, what it does to your mental state and how it affects everything and everyone around you. I will be sharing with you my personal experiences and pains, as well as those of my patients and others that I have witnessed, but more importantly, how I was able to put an end to these lies and now help others to do the same. This book is not a quick-fix guide or a book showcasing studies about depression, but instead the turning of each page is a catalyst moment as I share the truth about my journey with depression, with the hope that, even if only one life is saved by my story and message, then it has been worthwhile.

SCAN ME

1

CREATION

HOPE IS ALSO A STRATEGY

*"Never lose hope. Storms make people stronger
and never last forever."*
– Roy T Bennett

My story begins in Nigeria where I was the oldest in a family with eight siblings. We grew up in poverty, but it was not necessarily something that was apparent, because everyone was living in the same way in our village. My mother was a stay-at-home parent, the one who cared for our home and the children. When I was still young, my father joined the military, which meant that we left our home village to travel throughout our country. It was an amazing experience, as I learned so much about the different peoples and cultures that made up Nigeria.

My family had deep ties to our community, which involved a rich agricultural base. Throughout Africa, a beautiful and diverse continent, agriculture is the base of our cultures and communities.

I was born in a poor, backwater village named Fugar. Within this community, most of the people are hunters, fishermen, and farmers. Fugar, which is the collective name of two villages that make up the Avhianwu clan, is the administrative headquarters of Etsako, the local government of the Edo state.

These two villages are bonded socially, traditionally, and ancestrally with the sister villages of Ogbona and Ivhiraokho, remaining so down to this day. Historically, the name Fugar came from colonists, not the Avhianwu clan. These colonists made the connection between the young mature girls of marriageable age they found in that area upon landing there.

Back then, the young girls went around nude, wearing coral beads around their waists, and in some cases, a girl would adorn her body with beads from waist to chest. The girls were giants in height and second to none in the size of their busts. These young women were ready bait to any man, irrespective of his race.

The British colonialists and administrators cared for an area that became known as the Kukuruku Division with a large area of operation.

The problem was that they struggled to remember all the native names of the places found throughout this territory. While in formal settings, they would have those names written down, and in their casual conversations they found themselves associating places with striking characteristics. To be consistent, there had to be a formula and that was the vivid imagery of our beautiful country. Those beautiful girls were not seen as mature, young women, but full girls and our Kukuruku Division became known as the area of Full Girls. With the accents and intonation of colonists, it became OFUGA, a derivative of Full

Girls. Later, Ofuga was anglicised even further and eventually became known as Fugar. In this place of full girls, my father met his full girl, my mother, and I was born a year later between the chickens and cattle on a dry summer's day.

While my father was part of the military for much of my childhood, my grandfather was a traditional healer. I was exposed to various ways to serve my community, either through serving as a healer or a soldier. With the traveling from city to city that was part of my father's military life, I was exposed to a variety of languages and accents. I had to learn them quickly in order to adapt. Later in life, as I immigrated away from Nigeria, those skills came in handy.

I completed my secondary education within Nigeria and it came time to figure out what career I was going to pursue. For my parents, it had always been a struggle to make sure there was food on the table. When it came time to figure out what I was going to do for my future, my parents focus was making sure I did something that would always feed my family.

I could have become a professional footballer because I was very good at playing football. However, that career did not carry a high employment rate and one bad injury could have meant I was without a way to provide for myself and my family. Another option was to become a lawyer, but again, the legal profession in Nigeria did not offer job security or the stability my father wanted me to have in my professional career.

My father and grandfather both supported the idea of my becoming a doctor because of job security. It was seen as a noble profession, but one that would allow me to give back to my family and my home village. My father had always wanted to be a doctor himself, but it had not been possible. He projected his wish onto me, but I was okay with that because of watching my grandfather and seeing how he helped people. My grandfather originally thought I would become a traditional healer like him, but my father told him no, that I would become a real doctor, although still a part of the healing profession. No one really asked if I wanted to be a doctor, it was simply assumed that I would follow this path that would allow me to give back to my family, my siblings, and my home village. I was raised to serve others and it stuck with me as I entered the medical profession.

However, getting my medical education was going to be a challenge in Nigeria. I had studied all the necessary subjects in my secondary education to get into university, but I could not pay the school fees. The money to pay for that type of education was essentially out of reach for my family and community. However, there were opportunities for foreign exchange students to obtain scholarships and grants to receive their education abroad.

I started applying to different programs and multiple countries. There were applications and questions about the financial aid that I would receive but none of them resulted in the scholarships I needed to cover my university education. Finally, I received the news that I had been accepted into a program in Russia. My education would be paid for but I needed to pay for my travel costs to reach my new home. The costs of immigrating to Russia were out of reach for my family. Although I don't remember exactly how much the ticket cost back then, it was more money than we ever had.

Our only option was to reach out to the village and ask for donations. That meant asking church members, neighbours, companies, and more. Some people even sold part of their properties to help me pay for the trip. Everyone in the community contributed something because the understanding was that I would complete my education, then come back and provide services to the village. It was a contract that, in some way, I would elevate the community as a repayment for their communal financial sacrifice. That was a lot on my shoulders.

Once I left Nigeria, I realised that there was no way that I would be able to come back and practice medicine there. It would not be wise financially and therefore, I focused on working to gain knowledge and skills, in the hope that I would be able to send money back to the village and, in this way, fulfil my responsibility to them for their gift that ultimately allowed me to explore the world.

Arriving in Russia after a long train ride from the airport was a rude awakening. In Nigeria, we have grasslands and wetlands, and the dry and rainy seasons. The continent of Africa has never been known as a cold continent, therefore my country never experienced truly cold weather or snow.

Imagine walking off a train at age seventeen into a country known for its cold weather temperatures and having the equivalent of summer clothes only! I did not know the language, the customs, or anything about how Russia functioned. I went from living in a very agricultural-based, country community to a crowded city. Even the food options were different! Seeing snow for the first time was amazing because I had never seen anything like that before. It also meant I knew nothing about the different ways that the cold can affect your body.

When I had my first experience with frostbite, I actually thought someone was doing voodoo to me. My hands were tingling and it felt so painful. In Nigeria, fear of voodoo is a part of our culture and I truly thought that, if voodoo was being used on me, I was going to die right then and there! Needless to say, I didn't die. However, I made the mistake of putting my hands under hot water, something I will never do again!

Despite this dramatic change in my living conditions, I was excited to face challenges because I had fled the misery of poverty. The chances of falling prey to crime were greatly reduced because I was no longer in my home country, which was dealing with rampant criminality. People would do whatever they had to in order to provide for themselves and their families. I had escaped that cycle and was able to take another path.

There were still moments when I first arrived when I felt lonely because I didn't know anyone, feeling a little homesick for my family. Yet, there was a whole new world for me to explore. That was exciting for me! As I became acclimatised, the loneliness decreased because I was so busy meeting new people and learning new things.

Part of my early childhood experiences was being exposed to different languages and dialects as my family moved from place to place. In Africa, there are a variety of tribes and each one has a unique language. It is not uncommon for individuals to know a common tongue plus their tribal language. In fact, in Nigeria, there are three major languages, Igbo, Hausa, and Yoruba, as well as more than 390 minor languages with Edo being one of them. English is considered the official language in Nigeria and is widely used for communication in schools and the workplace. Yet, over three-quarters of the Nigerian population speaks two of the more popular languages in addition to English. This meant that I understood the process of learning a new language and found it to be a natural gift.

Still, I faced the unique challenge of learning the Russian language while trying to learn everything I needed to become a medical professional. Imagine being exposed to so many new words, phrases, sayings, and ideas in a new language. It was an exciting time and my curiosity and desire to learn thrived in this environment.

There were many individuals I met who opened their hearts and minds to me as a young, immigrant student. They would help me find the correct word in Russian, as well as introduce me to their amazing culture. My experience as a child who travelled due to my father's military career helped me to be open-minded to everything I was learning and the different interactions I had with so many people. It was also incredible to be fully immersed in a new language and culture. You definitely learn to communicate much faster when you simply have to.

I have seen individuals try to learn a language from books and tapes, but I think it slows the process down. Instead, finding ways to immerse yourself allows for a deeper and richer overall experience.

Plus, it was amazing for me to learn about how the body worked and to be exposed to a different level of health care than I had seen in my home country. These early experiences shaped how I viewed the medical world and what I could achieve for myself, if I was willing to put in the time and effort.

The first place I lived in Russia was a student hostel. Part of my Russian scholarship included covering my educational costs and providing me with somewhere to live. I was sharing a space with many people, but since I never had a room of my own at home, it was not a big adjustment.

Before this, I had never met someone from a foreign country. Now I was meeting people from 150 countries who spoke a variety of different languages. It was incredibly rewarding for me, exposing me to so much more than anatomy and knowledge of how to cure diseases.

Once I had As I finished my undergraduate work in Russia, the time came for me to decide where I would do my residency placement. While I had learned so much in Russia, I was also ready to leave the cold and explore something new. That meant applying for residencies in Europe, with the hope that I would be able to continue my education in another country. I was excited for new adventures in yet another place that was different from my home country.

Another benefit of going to Europe meant that I had more opportunities to earn money that I could send back home. It was a chance to help my family whilst exploring more places and cultures. Returning to Nigeria was not an option that I considered. I remembered the gruelling poverty and lack of job security. No way I thought. I had experienced all that poverty and I would not be part of it again. I looked for, and investigated, the possible options to advance my career and my sense of purpose. Thankfully, I was accepted into a psychology residency in the Netherlands, which was my opportunity to come to Europe to practise medicine. However, arriving in the Netherlands brought me some unique experiences.

On my arrival I had a hotel room booked for two nights. After that, I found myself homeless and on the streets. It was a vulnerable time, simply because being homeless puts you at a higher risk of doing drugs or committing a crime. I lived and roamed the streets of Amsterdam. I was a rolling stone, wherever I put my hat was my home. One day, I came into contact with Jerry, a forty-two year old pastor who told me that I didn't sound like a typical person who lived on the streets. He asked me about where I had come from and I explained my situation, including the fact that my immigration papers had expired. He helped me find a place to stay at a women's refugee camp. The women spoke Russian, and as I spoke both Russian and English, I was able to help them translate within their new world in the Netherlands. Due to my medical background, I was also able to go to the doctor with them and serve as a translator. I ended up staying there for about two months.

Then I met Henk and Ana who took me into their home and helped me learn the Dutch language. The number of languages that I could speak continued to grow. It was during this time that I met Anne, the future mother of my son. Relocating to the Netherlands meant learning a new system and I had to apply to medical school all over again. I had already spent many years studying in Russia and so having to repeat my studies again was very difficult for me. Yet, I never thought that my struggle had anything to do with depression. I thought that depression only happened to lazy people, not me. Depression is much more insidious and the truth is that there are so many lies we tell ourselves to avoid the reality of dealing with depression and its challenges.

In my country, the common idea is that depression does not exist. It is seen as a Western disease and it is a common misbelief that it is something that Africans do not suffer from. Our whole mindset is about moving forward. Mental health continues to be stigmatised, although that is now slowly changing. As I have learned over the years, there may be some truth to the fact that we are all prone to the possibility of suffering from depression at some point in our lives.

From an early age, I have always had a keen interest in spoken words and their power. I was also fascinated by how people use language to express their different states of mind.

Our beliefs are created in our minds. The words of Mahatma Gandhi come into play here: "Your beliefs become your thoughts, your thoughts become your words, your words become your actions, your actions become your habits, your habits become your values, your values become your destiny."

As part of my journey in the mental health field of medicine, I became fascinated with why people think the way that they think, and what triggers the thoughts that they have. Why are some individuals prone to grandiose thoughts and able to manifest them, while others are not?

The truth is that life has a deadline that all of us will meet at some point. During that timeline, some of us may become mentally sick. Why is that the case for some of us, but not for others? If how we think is how we act, then it is clear that our thoughts and the words we use have a lot of power to transform our lives.

I developed this interest in mental health care even further during my residency as a general practitioner. I was also fortunate enough to work with my supervisor and watch him literally transforming thoughts. It was the power of words in action.

My interest in mental health also resulted from my own personal experience with depression, although I didn't really understand depression until I was dealt a critical loss.

Depression can be hard to recognise in yourself, even if the signs are there. Excuses are easy to come up with and you can justify why you are struggling mentally. I know this first hand because I finally admitted to myself that there was something going on, something more than grief.

I was working in my medical residency (placement), supporting my siblings financially and doing what I could to help my family by working hard to learn and grow in my chosen profession. My relationship with my dad was great, we were very close a close one, as I learned so much from him about how to care for and lead the family. On the other hand, my relationship with my mother was not as close. I struggled to communicate with her and I often felt as if we couldn't understand one another's point of view.

My father was in a tragic accident and, for two weeks, we wondered if he would survive. I had been keeping up with the news from Nigeria whilst I was in the Netherlands. Then on May 2nd 2017, I received the call that rocked my world. It was 8:00 am and I was walking through one of the corridors of the Westend Hospital in the Hague, one of the largest hospitals in the Netherlands. About twenty metres in front of me was an elderly couple walking slowly and holding hands. Directly opposite us was the hospital pharmacy with its long queue and ahead was a signpost directing you to the General Practice. On the left was a bookshop and flower shop, where families could buy cards and flowers to cheer their loved ones who were in hospital.

Outside, construction workers continued a building project creating a new location for the emergency department. The windows along the corridor allowed the fresh summer sun to shine into the spaces throughout the hospital. The traffic sounds from the busy, metropolitan city of The Hague were also present. It was bustling and full of life.

I remember it clearly, like a snapshot in time because of the news that I received moments later.

My iPhone started ringing in my back pocket, the ringing persisted It was persistent but I didn't want to pick it up because

I feared the news I would hear from the person on the other end of that call.

"Hello Kracavitza," I said, using one of my pet names for my partner of thirteen years, Genia. "I have been trying to call you," she said. "Your Uncle Law, who lives in Belgium, has been trying to reach you too. He couldn't reach you, so he called me. He wanted to tell you himself. I hate to be the one to deliver this news." In her characteristic, calm and gentle voice, as kindly as she could, she said, "I am sorry, my angel. Papa is gone. Papa is not there anymore. Papa is dead. I am sorry."

I can only imagine how painful and agonising it must have been for her to be the one to tell me that news. Genia wasn't even able to comfort me in person, so it must have felt even worse, although she tried to do her best over the phone.

The world froze and as the words sunk into my brain, it seemed as if time just stopped. I could see images of everyone around me, but nothing appeared real. Only two-dimensional characters moved past me. I stood in the middle of the hallway, feeling as if my feet were nailed to the ground. Every part of me felt heavy, as though all my energy and ability to move had drained away.

The telephone in my right hand felt strange, as if it was there, but lacked substance. The words of my partner echoed throughout my head and heart. I am sorry. Papa is dead. Papa is dead. I am sorry. Papa is dead.

It was the moment that I had hoped and prayed was never going to happen, yet now I was standing there and hearing those dreaded words. The tragic accident had taken another victim, my father. My world was shattered!

What was I going to do now?

My father was the head of our family, my mentor, and my best friend. He had been a man of peace and wisdom. I found myself in a state of denial. He wasn't gone, I kept telling myself. No, he is not gone. I don't remember hanging up my phone or moving out of the corridor, but eventually I did.

Soon I received a call from Nigeria, confirming what I had already been told. Before that call, I denied the truth in my head and heart by telling myself that he was still alive and that there was still some hope. I found a place to sit in the hospital and I felt a calmness settle upon me. That calmness told me he wasn't gone yet. He would soon recover. Whatever was within my ability to send, in terms of the best material and financial assistance, I sent it to the medical team back in Nigeria.

I had been working tirelessly to send financial assistance home. There was no way that all of that effort was in vain. He couldn't leave me now. My mind rebelled at the thought. My father was larger than life and my hero. Heroes do not leave the world this way. But, that calmness was shattered by the piping sound notifying me of a text message from my brother, Harry on the other phone in my left back pocket.

Papa is dead, read the text.

All those hopes that I had been cultivating in my head were dashed. At only 69, a few months before his 70th birthday in October, my father was dead. All my plans of giving him a grand surprise for his birthday celebration were dashed. It would never come to be. I cried out to God, asking Him why the good ones of the world leave so early.

To understand the profound impact this would have on my life, I have to share a part of our traditions regarding family. My father was the head of our family, but as the oldest child,

I was taught to bear a lot of responsibility on my shoulders. Everyone in the family looks up to you. When the father or head of the family passes away, the oldest son takes over the responsibilities of a father in literally every conceivable way. My father had been my shield for a long time, allowing me to circumvent the responsibilities of being his oldest son. I love my brothers and sisters dearly, but it was nice to know that I didn't have to give them all the answers. I could address financial worries, but my father had a masterly way of playing around and soothing everyone's feelings, even if their problems were not actually solved.

Now that responsibility fell to me.

I had to rise to the occasion. I first called my brother, Goddy, who was immediately my junior and a sibling to whom I felt extremely close. We spoke extensively. Then I worked my way through all of my siblings, giving them each a call and speaking with them about our loss. Finally, my mother was the last one left. I needed to speak with my mother, but I couldn't. Every time I called, I was told that she was in shock and disbelief.

I wondered if speaking with her right now was even going to be effective. Our relationship was built on my respect for her, but I felt that it was shallow. I didn't know how to communicate with her. Most of our conversations didn't last five minutes. My father had served as the bridge between us. He had shared with me that my mother didn't know how to communicate with me either.

She believed I had been gone from home for so long that I was out of her reach and wouldn't understand the messages she wanted to relay to me. Now our bridge was gone, and we had to figure out how to talk with each other. What would I say to her?

For now, I was happy that she was being cared for by my siblings in Nigeria. I realised the truth that there was power in numbers. I had given them all the emotional support and consolation as the new head of the family. Now it was my turn to receive emotional support and consolation.

I took my phone out and dialled the number to call my mentor, friend, and confidante.

There was silence at the other end of the phone. I listened to the voicemail message, feeling grateful to have someone to speak to when times are hard. Then I realised that he would never call me back. Life would never be the same. For the first time since I had received that initial call from my partner, tears rolled down my cheeks. The last time I cried this intensely was seventeen years ago when my son was born. I had been so happy, excited, and joyful as I became a father. Now I had lost mine.

For the next two days, I was still unable to speak to my mother. Fear was gripping me at night. I knew that there was something that my family in Nigeria was not telling me about my mother. I was furiously calling home but kept hearing that she was okay and mute. Different thoughts crept into my brain. I wondered how she was going to cope with all of this. She had been with my father since she was fifteen and now her husband was gone after nearly fifty years together.

Supporting my siblings had been worthwhile and I thought I was managing this terrible loss well enough, considering everything I had to juggle.

Then out of the blue, on the highway home, it hit me hard that my hero was gone. Out of those dark skies that night, a darkness descended upon me. Tears rolled out of my eyes and down my cheeks. Where was this coming from? I felt troubled at my reaction. It filled me with confusion, fear, and panic about where this was going to lead. Would I be able to stand up for my family? I had to be physically, mentally, and emotionally fit for them now. My whole family was resting on me and emotionally I was doing well, or so I thought.

Three months later I was driving home at 2:00 am after a regular night shift. The weeks had been very busy and intensive. It was dark and lonely on the highway, which depicted the precise state of my being. Darkness and loneliness. The contents of my mind were darker than the darkness outside the confines of my car. Gently, like a thief in the night, that idea which I had been able to push away through the previous weeks crept into my mind. What is the essence of it all? I will die anyway. I will die young anyway. I have felt convinced about this.

What is the essence of it all? This doom and darkness, this feeling of hopelessness and helplessness is crushing. It is too much. Who cares anyway if I am not there anymore. How am I going to take care of my mother, my siblings and the community? I am hopeless, I feel hopeless and helpless. I am helpless and stupid. Above all, I am tired. I am exhausted. I wake up exhausted, I go to bed exhausted. My whole body hurts, There is an ever-persistent lump on my chest. I wonder how I am driving this car right now. Slowly, the darkness of the thoughts, like the darkness outside the car engulfed me. This is my moment, I said to myself, this is the moment. I am the only one on the highway. The darkness of my thoughts is still darker than the darkness of the night. I will do no one harm, This is my moment. That voice and idea which had been lingering all this while was growing. *OK go for it, this is it. You can finally bid farewell. You will feel peace of mind. First, you will feel pain, but then, darkness and loneliness no more. You will be liberated from it all. Finally. At last.*

I glanced at the speedometer, and pressed down more on the gas pedal. Gradually the speedometer increased: 100km/u, 120/km, 140km/u, 160 km... *Go on, faster, faster faster, faster faster, you are almost there, hit the rails, this will be quick. It's not going to be painful.* My heart was palpitating, my fingertips were trembling, sweat covered my forehead. My knees felt heavy, my stomach felt empty. That chest tightness was constant. Anyway, I told myself, *you will be free soon.* Finally free from the build up of pain, anger, frustrations and guilt. Oh finally. *Yes, that is the tree I am heading and driving forward to.* I have seen that tree many times before and have made some silent mental notes to her. I have been having this idea, that the tree is beckoning me to come to her. I do not feel the tightness of my chest anymore. All of a sudden the chest tightness has gone. *See, I am moving in the right direction. The chest pain has gone. When all this is over I won't feel any pain anymore. Pain of guilt. Failure. Shame. All will be gone.* Finally. My mind was racing and, about ten seconds before the tree, my car stopped. The tears rolled down my cheeks. I didn't want to die after all. Ten seconds. The tears started flowing. *What are you doing?* Shame and anguish engulfed me.

What are you doing Ikhenemoh, what are you doing? Hot tears flooded my cheeks, blurring my vision. I was shaken. I cried out like a wounded lion who had abandoned his family. I was woken by a knock at the window of my car, the next morning. A policeman asked me to wind down the car window. The neighbours had noted a strange car in the neighbourhood and the owners of the nearby fuel station wanted the car to leave. The realisation hit me. I had slept the whole night in my car. I didn't hear clearly what the policeman was telling me. His voice sounded as if it was from afar. His clear, blue eyes pierced into me as he handed me back my driving licence. As I took hold of my driver's licence I felt as if he was giving me back permission to live. I would see another day, I thought. I am alive. I get to see any day. Every day above the ground is a great day. I am here. I am alive. I am alive!

In the confines of my car, I became honest with myself. I couldn't keep pretending that I was doing well. There was no stopping the tears. Author, Jamie Anderson said it best. Grief, I have learnt, is love with no place to go. It's all the love you want to give but cannot. All that unspent love gathers up in the corners of your eyes, the lump in your throat and that hollow part of your chest. Grief is just love with no place to go. I needed to break out of my piled-up emotions, but I believed that I needed to handle it all on my own. I was determined that I would. Every man is born with a purpose. What was my purpose?

Every day above the ground is a great day.

Fast forward two weeks later. I was at a three-day event called the A Factor. On the first day as you walk towards the hall you can hear the music and capture the excitement in the air. I wondered to myself, is this yet another of those feel good events where you become pumped up, return home, and then what?

The speaker was introduced to the stage.

In the final hour there was a Q&A. I listened attentively and took notes as he answered the questions of the attendees. Finally, I raised my hand and behold he saw me. The following conversation ensued:

Me: My name is Ikhenemoh and I am worried.

Him: What are you worried about? Tell me more.

Me. I am worried about my mother. Who is going to take care of her? I relayed the story of my upbringing and the events of the last three months. I omitted my attempt to kill myself two weeks ago. I was too ashamed to talk about that and certainly not to these people who I didn't know. He listened patiently and, at the time, was applying what I later came to know as NLP (Neuro-linguistic Programming). I felt calm and reassured, until the last part of our conversation:

Him: How old are you?

Me: 43

Him: You are not young anymore. Sit down and stop telling yourself that. The hall burst into laughter. I guessed I was craving sympathy.

You are not young anymore, so stop craving sympathy and stop with that self-pity. For the next two days, his words lingered in my ears along with the laughter in the hall.

At that moment, I decided the time for self pity was gone. It was time for action. Every day above the ground is a great day. I listened to powerful people like Wayne Dyer, Tony Robbins, and Les Brown. I became immersed in Holocaust survivor Viktor Frankl's classic book, Man's Search for Meaning. I started attending seminars.

My certainty in who I was, and a false sense of security had been swept away. I had been living the life of a great pretender, putting on a pretence that I was doing well with my loss. I needed to become the true person that I was meant to be. The question was, how was I going to break through the pretending?

Grief is just love with no place to go.

As I write this I look back at the quote a friend sent me the other day and the photograph of the man which I have on my desk, whose death has changed my life. Life will never be the same again. There is going to be a very painful moment in your life that will change your entire world in a matter of minutes. These moments will change you. Let them make you stronger, smarter, kinder. But, don't go and become someone that you aren't. *Cry*. Scream if you have to. Then you straighten out that crown and keep moving. Last night, on the highway, was a defining moment for me. The morning at the A Factor was another moment as I heard the laughter in the room. I needed no sympathy, I needed strength. I had been looking for the wrong thing. I would not do self pity anymore.

Although I didn't know it at the time, I was suffering from depression. The truth was, I was in denial that it could happen to me. I was an African and believed that 'depression is a Western disease.' That is a lie. I had patients with depression, but I was not a patient. I had dealt with stress and suffered through hard times, but I had not fallen victim to depression. That was a lie.

I had seen the toll that depression took on my patients first hand and always thought 'that could never happen to me.' That was a lie. I told myself that everybody has sad days and days with low mood. I was having sad days, but not depression. Depression is a lie because it makes you believe all these reasons why it cannot happen to you. Shock and denial can make it hard to accept that you are dealing with depression. People who knew me as an upbeat optimist started wondering what was wrong with me. While I dealt with my depression, it gave me a deeper insight into what my patients were dealing with, and what could be keeping them from dealing with it. Those suffering from depression often find it hard to admit that they need help.

Over the years, I have found a few common reasons why people struggle to reach out for help and deal with their depression effectively.

Denial – So many individuals, including myself, have a pre-conceived picture of what depression looks and feels like, making it easy for them to deny what is happening right in front of them. They avoid asking for help because they think they don't need it.

Shame – Depression is seen as a weakness and only few people like to admit that they have any weakness. They feel that there is shame associated with admitting that they need help, or that they are struggling with depression.

Misconceptions – It can't happen to you because… (fill in the blank). People have so many cultural, social, and family expectations that it can be hard to admit they have depression. Worse still, they might have misconceptions that make them believe depression can only seem one way, when it can show up in a variety of different ways.

SEVEN COMMON MISCONCEPTIONS

Depression is a sign of weakness

Depression can affect anyone, regardless of physical or mental strength. Some of the world's most well-known citizens – including Abraham Lincoln, Winston Churchill, Mozart, Isaac Newton, J.K. Rowling to mention a few - have experienced depression. I don't have a sense that these great minds are weak people. People who are battling depression are strong. They fight every single day and they wake up each morning and have to fight again.

External stressors – All of us deal with stress, but the truth is that our minds have a limit to how much they can take. Eventually, too much stress through external stressors can end up pushing us mentally to the brink and that can leave us vulnerable to depression.

It's all in your head

Some people deny the fact that depression is a real illness. The truth is that depression is a legitimate, medical condition related to brain chemistry, function, structure, and sometimes involves environmental or biological factors. Symptoms of depression can include aches and pains, disturbed sleeping patterns and extreme lethargy. It causes feelings of hopelessness, sadness, and self-doubt. Suicidal thoughts are not uncommon. It's important to know that depression is treatable and that recovery is possible.

Depression only affects women

Our culture sometimes discourages men from discussing their feelings, asking for help or showing signs of weakness. As a result, some men turn away from treatment. Men are three times more likely to die by suicide than women. If you are a man experiencing depression, or have thoughts of suicide, know that you are not alone. According to research done by the National Institute of Mental Health, approximately six million American men go through depression each year. Suicide is the leading cause of death among men under the age of thirty-five. Our culture must acknowledge the importance of mental health treatment for everyone who needs it, and this includes men.

People with depression are ungrateful and lazy

This one I literally heard this morning, A family member was describing a sibling who should be grateful because of all the sacrifices her parents have made for her education. People may have numerous things to be grateful about in their life, but still experience depression. Claiming that someone is ungrateful for feeling depressed because they have things in their life can make that person feel even more ashamed. Others claim that depression is simply an excuse for laziness. This is a harmful myth as the reality is that depression affects some people in a way that they become fatigued, to the point that they are unable to finish simple tasks.

Talking about it only makes it worse

Try not to ignore the symptoms of depression if you see it in your spouse, children or co-workers. Showing support can be very valuable for the person going through depression. It is a relief when someone notices a change in your mood or behaviour and has the compassion and courage to ask how you're doing. Friends and family members can be very helpful to a person experiencing depression, by listening and offering steady support and encouragement.

The best way to help someone with depression is to try and cheer them up

Well-meaning people will often tell a person with depression to look on the bright side, snap out of it, or stop thinking about it. However, it's much more complicated than that. The best way to help a person with depression is to make sure they have access to screening and treatment. A depression screening can be done during a primary care visit, during an intake appointment at a counselling centre, or in the privacy of your home with a confidential call to a crisis hotline.

It's fashionable these days to say you have depression

Despite, or perhaps, due to the COVID pandemic, talking more openly about mental health has become easier. Some people believe that it is trendy to say you have depression. My observation is that the stigma of depression will gradually be lifted. All too frequently the term depression tends to be thrown around as being sad or in a low mood. We have to understand that depression is more than sadness, but a condition that shouldn't be taken lightly.

Let's look more closely at the most prevailing signs and symptoms of depression:

- Feelings of hopelessness which can affect the way you look at life. This is the most common sign of depression.

- Loss of interest: lacking joy comes with depression. Losing interest in activities that were once enjoyed.

- Increased fatigue and sleep problems: sleepiness during daytime hours or other sleep issues, including insomnia.

- Anxiety: although depression doesn't exactly cause anxiety, these two conditions can occur at the same time. In his fascinating book, Reasons to Stay Alive, Matt Haig observed that the combination of anxiety with depression is the most common mental illness in the UK, followed by anxiety, post traumatic stress disorder, pure depression, phobias, eating disorders, OCD and panic disorders.

- Irritability: research shows that men with depression may have symptoms such as irritability, escapist or risk behaviour, substance abuse or misplaced anger.

- Changes in appetite and weight: some people suffering from depression may have an increase in appetite and gain weight whilst others experience appetite loss and may lose weight.

- Uncontrollable emotions: depression can cause mood swings which are difficult to control and happen irregularly, or with certain triggering factors.

- Looking at death: depression can be connected with the desire to stop living or give up on life when things become difficult to bear.

In his thought-provoking book, The Inflamed Mind: A Radical New Approach to Depression, Cambridge Professor, Edward Bullmore, explains the latest science behind a new theory linking depression to inflammation of the body. While I believe that there is emerging evidence for this line of thinking,

I feel that more research has to be done to explore this route of thinking. Inflammation as a possible underlying cause of depression is not a myth, as others may suggest, and does not fall into the category of misconception.

Clearly, there are many factors which contribute to why people struggle to identify that they have depression, and then to seek help to address it. As I worked with my patients and gained a greater understanding of depression through my own experiences, I realised that there are five areas in which a person can potentially fall into depression.

For some who are close to me, there are parts of this book that may come as a surprise to you - I get that. It is no fault of yours that I didn't come to you earlier. This is the lie that depression tells you: that nobody will understand you. Now, I know better.

This idea came about in October 2019, during an initial conversation with my mentor, Jessen Chinnapan, whom I first met at the seminar, Power to Achieve, where he was a guest speaker. He talked about mindset and using your story to help others. You can do this in different ways: like setting up your own business or writing a book. I signed onto one of Jessen's programmes.

During our first mentorship meeting, I remember Jessen saying, "If you don't share your story, so others may learn from it, you are selfish." You can call me anything you like, and you will probably be right, but selfish is not one of them. One day, you too will tell your story of how you overcame what you are going through now, and it will become part of somebody else's survival guide. Three years later, I have summoned the courage to write the words you are reading. As I listened to Jessen, I wanted to know him better.

When all is said and done, I recollect the words of a young mother who was battling with depression once saying to me, "Because of you, I didn't give up." At that moment, it all felt worth it. Happiness.Doctor was conceived and the idea to write this book was born.

> ## "Hope and fear cannot occupy the same space. Invite one to stay."
> – Maya Angelou

Hope, sometimes that's all that you have, when you have nothing at all. If you have hope, you have everything. I was driving home from a night shift and listening to a conversation between a high-performance coach and a high-flying CEO telling each other that hope is not a good strategy. They were trying to explain that you must have a solid business plan, and not just hope for the best. I shared this line of thought with my colleagues, and from my experience, many of them agree with this practical view. However, after my depression and looking at it from a survivor's perspective, increasingly I found myself saying, "Hope is probably the best strategy." Hope, in combination with faith, that all will be well and that too shall pass is a very potent outlook for sailing through this storm and battle called depression. At the time of writing, as people, organisations and businesses face the challenge of COVID-19, and many are feeling low and starting to despair, the best way to give support is to help them see that there is hope.

And there is HOPE.

I hope I can see my family soon. I hope I can keep my job. I hope I will be able to see my sick mother. I hope my business survives. I hope I get paid this month.

I hope we don't have to cancel our wedding.

I hope I can say farewell to my Dad.

I hope I'm home for Christmas.

I hope we don't go into lockdown again.

I hope I don't catch this virus.

Right now, many people are feeling confused and helpless, and now, more than ever, the one thing they need is a sense of hope. If someone is struggling, we must be there for them and reassure them. We may not be able to promise them anything like the points on the list above, but by showing consideration and kindness, we will give them hope that someone cares.

Draw hope from how you have got through difficult situations in the past. Take hope from the people who want you to survive and thrive. No matter how bad it gets, see hope in the practical steps we can take to improve the quality of life and save lives.

I have always resonated with this:

"Hope is not blind optimism. It's not ignoring the enormity of the task ahead or the roadblocks that stand in our path. It's not sitting on the sidelines or shirking from a fight. Hope is that thing inside us that insists, despite all evidence to the contrary, that something better awaits us if we have the courage to reach for it, and to work for it, and to fight for it. Hope is the belief that destiny will not be written for us, but by us, by the men and women who are not content to settle for the world as it is, who have the courage to remake the world as it should be."
— Barack Obama

COGNITION

2

POWER OF THE MIND

"Your beliefs become your thoughts, your thoughts become your words, your words become your actions, your actions become your habits, your habits become your values, your values become your destiny."
– Mahatma Gandhi

Mental illness always has been, and still is, a sore subject, a condition that carries shame and a trail of damage behind it, as at times it can lead to an individual being sectioned in a mental institution, or even worse, death by suicide. The pain does not only affect the one with the condition, but also those around them. The question that will always be at the top of one's head is…

WHAT CAUSES DEPRESSION?

For a long time, society did not recognise the fact that depression can affect anyone, regardless of age, culture, lifestyle, or family history. There are numerous factors that can impact mental health, including biology, environment, challenges and traumatic life events. There is no single cause, and it is not anyone's fault. This is the reality of the situation.

There was a time when society wanted depression to be downplayed and seen as unhappiness, rather than as a matter of the mind - a mental illness. This lack of acknowledgement meant that a crucial part of human stability was ignored: everything else would be highlighted for improvement, but the mind and its power were overlooked.

Throughout the journey of life, I have come to learn that the mind is indeed a powerful tool, when used properly. For one to understand partly how important the mind is, it may be necessary for me to share an analogy relating to one of our modern day cars. Let's take a look at one of the most luxurious cars in today's age, the Tesla, known for its modern designs, innovative technology and high performance. Take the Model S, for instance, which features full self-driving capability and additional features, such as auto lane changing, the ability to automatically retrieve your car and automated parking, amongst other sophisticated perks, which are all achievable due to the brain embedded within the vehicle.

Now, I want you to think about having one of these vehicles parked in your drive, but without a brain or the computer board needed to send out the signals, which activate the features and even make driving the car possible. What value would it then have? What is eccentric about the car is not the shell of the body, no matter how strong and beautiful it is, but the brain of the vehicle, which passes the information to the functionality of the car. Therefore, it is clear that without the brain, the Tesla loses its value and power. It is the same with us as human beings. Having a beautiful, healthy or strong physique is worth nothing if your mental capacity is not in the right state. This is an area where many go wrong as they determine the well-being of others or themselves based on their outward appearance. This is something that I will explore further in this chapter.

WHAT IS COGNITION?

Cognition is a term referring to the mental processes involved in gaining knowledge and comprehension. These processes include thinking, knowing, remembering, judging, and problem solving, all higher-level functions of the brain. Most people tend to believe that their brain and mind are the same, however, the brain is an organ, whilst the mind is not. We could say the brain is the physical place where the mind resides. It is a vessel in which the electronic impulses that create thought are contained. With the brain you coordinate your moves, your organism, your activities and transmit impulses, whereas the mind is used to think. You can muse at what has happened, what is scheduled and what maybe will happen.

The mind is the manifestation of thought, emotion, determination, memory, perception and imagination that takes place within the brain. Mind is often used to refer especially to the thought processes of reason. The mind is the awareness of consciousness, the ability to control what we do, and know what we are doing and why, the ability to understand.

Imagine your head is a computer that controls everything you do, your brain being the physical hardware box which has all the power connections, storage, memory, electrical wiring, and the processing power you need to function as a human being. Then, think about the mind being the software, the operating system which gathers, stores, and manages information, using the massive processing resources of your brain. Therefore, in reality, your brain and your mind are inseparable, they are of the same entity, one cannot operate without the other. Your thoughts are generated by your mind, which as I mentioned, is like your brain's software. However, your mind has different layers of consciousness.

THE CONSCIOUS MIND

Scientists believe that your conscious mind makes up less than ten percent of the mind's total operational power and is responsible for:

- Gathering data
- Assessing and processing the data you are collecting
- Finding patterns and making comparisons
- Making decisions and giving orders
- The ability to respond thoughtfully to situations
- Controlling your short-term memory

When something is in your conscious mind, it is deliberate and you are 'aware' of it.

THE UNCONSCIOUS MIND

The remaining ninety percent of your 'software' is your unconscious mind. It feels inaccessible, because you are not consciously aware of what goes on in there, but, be assured, your unconscious mind is immensely powerful.

- It operates the body, including breathing, digestion, sleeping, heart rate and temperature control, all without you having to lift a finger (and it controls that too).

- It protects you by trying to maintain the status quo, which is why you sometimes feel uncomfortable when making a change. Your unconscious mind wants to steer you back to what is familiar and therefore, 'safe'.
- It is the seat of your emotions.
- It is the origin of your imagination and creativity.
- It is where your habits are created and maintained – I'll come back to that in a minute.
- It follows instructions from your conscious mind.
- It causes you to react automatically when something threatens you – you might run or freeze or as your fight or flight response kicks in.
- It stores and retrieves longer term memories.

WHY IS IT IMPORTANT TO UNDERSTAND HOW YOUR MIND WORKS?

Ultimately, this knowledge gives you greater control over how to use the combined power of your conscious and unconscious mind to think in a more healthy, flexible, resilient, and goal-supporting way. The benefits include improved self-worth, far less emotional upheaval, and a much greater ability to achieve what you want in life. When I learnt this, it was a massive game changer for me. As you can tell from my story, a lack of knowledge led me to believe the lies and made me fall victim to my circumstances at the time.

One function of the unconscious mind is to create and maintain habits. It is a known fact that our mind forms habits both good and bad, and the more knowledgeable you are, you can use this to your advantage.

I didn't always know the importance and power of my mind, until I fell victim to depression and it was almost too late. To be honest, I did not recognise what was happening to me, or even want to be stigmatised with the word 'depression', thinking that it was taboo and I was just unhappy. I used to tell myself, "I am a strong, healthy man and depression is for those who are weak." That shows you how much I knew, but it was a real issue for me. In reality, I was like a drunk man claiming not to be drunk.

I found that the greatest challenge for most individuals, whether it be patients, friends, or even myself, was being unable to accept that something was wrong, a real problem.

ACKNOWLEDGING THE PROBLEM

One of the first things that stands in the way of anyone addressing their depression is recognising what they are dealing with. When I was suffering from depression, it took me a while to admit what it was. I was an African, a Nigerian, and we did not get depressed. That only happened to other people. My thoughts were focused on my cultural beliefs, which made me deny the evidence that was right in front of me.

Eventually, however, I could no longer deny my reality. I finally saw and acknowledged the problem. Breaking out of the denial phase is difficult, but without doing so, you will be unable to help yourself. Once I acknowledged my depression, it opened my mind to search for solutions. Instead of continuing to feel bad, I concentrated on finding the light at the end of the tunnel. Problems have solutions and can be fixed, but when an individual is in denial, little progress can be made.

Denial is easy to fall into because many of us have a dire picture of depression. This might include someone being unable to get out of bed, unable to take care of themselves, and constantly sad. The truth is that depression can impact a wide variety of people and create different issues for each individual. When I was depressed, I was still getting up every day and going to work. I was still functioning in society and caring for myself physically. Yet, mentally, grief was overwhelming me.

Perhaps you find yourself still caring for various aspects of life but doing so with a heavy cloud over your head. Everything that you are doing may feel like a burden. Acknowledging the problem means understanding that this is not the way you want to live, and it is not normal.

Another part of recognising your depression means accepting what is happening in your life. Although you may not like it, you cannot continue to deny that it is happening or act as though it is not there. Here are a few of the circumstances that you might be facing:

- Are you having problems in your relationships?
- Are there stresses at work that are building up and having a negative impact?
- Have you lost a loved one to death?
- Are you dealing with a life-threatening illness, or even a chronic one?
- Are you caring for a loved one who is dealing with a life-threatening illness or a chronic one?

Situations such as these can cause a high level of mental and emotional stress. Depression can start to set in when you are dealing with challenging circumstances and feeling as if there is nothing you can do to change them.

These negative thoughts and mindset can trap you in a spiral that will only magnify your depression. Instead, acknowledge your circumstances and then focus on what you want to change right now. It might be a small thing, but you will feel better having acted, instead of allowing your thoughts to continue in a negative cycle.

Acknowledgement of the problem also means that you can reach out for help from others, be it your support system or medical professionals. Still, there is much that you can do on your own to help yourself in dealing with depression. One of the first things that you have the power to change is your attitude. Let's talk about what that means.

"Until you give your dog a name, it's not yours. If you don't label it, then you don't own it, if you don't own it, then you can't solve it. A call that has not been made cannot be answered." – John Risner.

> ## A call that has not been made cannot be answered."
> – John Risner.

You are holding this book in your hands and have come this far because something intrinsic in you is telling you that there is an issue you would like to resolve. You are not alone.

You have accomplished some things, yet you are not fulfilled. Where is this feeling coming from? How long have you had this feeling? How long do you want to feel this way? Another week, a month, a year? Are you in a state of denial like the great pretender, wearing your hat like a crown? It's time to dig, and tap into the space and silence where answers will be found. Questions will be asked and answers, uncomfortable answers, will come. Sometimes, we may think that one has to be in a ditch, tucked away under the sheets or having constant failures to become depressed, but that is not the case at all. Even some of the highest achievers are suffering in silence. The question is, could that also be you?

ACCEPTING THE PROBLEM

You may be asking, "Dr Ikhenemoh, are acknowledgement and acceptance not the same thing?" As the brain and the mind differ whilst being the same entity, likewise for acknowledgement and acceptance. The difference is that acceptance is to approve or receive the truth, whilst acknowledgement is to recognise and embrace the truth.

Your next thought may be, "Now that I have asked the questions and the answers have come, what should I do with them?" Now that you have given the dog a name, it is yours– you have ownership, you have labelled the problem. So now what? Why do I call it labelling? I know that for some, the term 'labelling' has negative connotations. Labelling the problem is all about taking the first step to experience the journey to freedom, and to reclaim your life.

It all begins by consciously understanding what depression is and naming it. Accepting that there is a problem can be extremely hard, and finally realising and knowing its name can be twice as hard. However, at the same time, this knowledge enables you to obtain the assistance needed. One of the reasons why some prefer depression to remain unnamed is because of the shame and stigma which are sometimes attached to it. This brings me to one of the most common misconceptions of depression as a sign of weakness, as I mentioned earlier.

Far from signifying weakness, depression is a real medical condition, like diabetes, high blood pressure, asthma, or cancer. Depression is not a test of character or strength. It is not temporary, nor will it go away by itself. In actuality, it is a medical condition that requires treatment and support. Therefore, it is important to seek help early to prevent symptoms from getting worse. Accepting that there is a problem is a crucial part of the whole process. This comes with the realisation that something is wrong and that a choice must be made between doing nothing and neglecting the problem, or fixing it. Doing nothing is also a choice. It is not an ideal choice, but a choice anyhow. You may tell yourself that you hate the way you are feeling, so why accept it? Isn't that giving in to hopelessness and helplessness? Imagine you had cancer. Would you not agree that you cannot start treatment without knowing the condition's name, so that you can accept that it is cancer and define its stage?

The longer you wait for treatment, the less chance you have for survival. Accepting that you have cancer is the first step on the journey to beat it. Depression is no different. Naming, labelling, and accepting that you are going through depression means that you are giving yourself a chance to overcome it. You must accept an addiction, and its power over you, before you can find the humility to fight it. Likewise, you must accept depression before you can learn how to deal with it and break free from its bondage.

> "Acceptance means no complaining, and happiness means no complaining about the things over which you can do nothing."
> – Wayne Dyer

ATTITUDE

Once you have acknowledged and accepted that you, or someone you know, is actually suffering from depression, a change of attitude is required to move forward in the right direction. As a doctor, I have seen many that have been diagnosed with a condition and expect that they will heal or recover with the same attitude and habits that got them into that state in the first place. You cannot keep putting your hands into a wasps' nest, expecting that you will not be stung. How can you carry on doing the same thing, but expect different outcomes? As the great Albert Einstein stated, this is the definition of insanity, which you definitely want to avoid.

Therefore, acknowledgment and acceptance are only the beginning of the long journey to recovery. The next step is to address your attitude concerning your condition, environment, and coping mechanisms. Attitude has a great deal to do with what you are feeling right now. Your thoughts and emotions are the main factors that affect your mental health. Negative attitudes, and feelings of helplessness and hopelessness, can create chronic stress, which upsets the body's hormone balance, depletes the brain chemicals required for happiness, and damages the immune system.

It is important to recognise our thoughts and emotions and to be aware of their effect not solely on each other, but also on our bodies, behaviour, and relationships. This means that your attitude contributes to the entire success of your recovery. Your attitude is what will determine how you go through your daily life, your outlook, thought processes and actions.

Alongside my experience, study has shown that depression is a mood disorder characterised by profound feelings of sadness, isolation, hopelessness, or emptiness. It can be so overwhelming that it prevents you from enjoying things which once interested you. Depression affects everyone differently and has the ability to interfere with daily activities, work, and life in general.

Taking the time to analyse or seek help in recognising your attitude can assist in your knowing the areas where you may need help and the coping mechanisms which you may need. It is also very important to establish the right people and environment that have the best attitude towards your illness, as this can have a major effect on your condition. Treating depression is so much more than therapy and taking medication. Changing your attitude will, in turn, give you the ability to change your lifestyle to ensure a healthier mind and body, enabling you to cope with the challenges of depression.

Focusing on your attitude will lead you to concentrate on your habits or daily activities. This will indeed take much effort, but is necessary for recovery. You may not have anticipated that I would touch on this, especially as I know firsthand how difficult it is to dig yourself out of the big, dark hole into which depression plunges you. I appreciate and can totally relate, but burying your head in the sand is only giving depression the permission to take over your life.

Further on, I mention some areas that will be beneficial for you to focus on, areas that the lies of depression would want to tell you not to do. Your attitude right now may be more towards lying in bed and pulling the sheet over your head, yes I totally get that. However, you have to remind yourself that your attitude towards your condition will determine how well you will be able to overcome the challenges of depression. As the saying goes, how you do anything is how you do everything.

DO YOU AGREE?

Attitude is defined as "a settled way of thinking or feeling about someone or something, typically one that is reflected in a person's behaviour." If you are dealing with depression, without acknowledging it, then your attitude has settled into a way of thinking that is ignoring your mental and emotional suffering. However, once you acknowledge your situation and how depression is impacting you, then you can see how it is also affecting your attitude. Without the right attitude, you deny yourself the power to change your thoughts. Shifting your attitude can often start by changing your thoughts, even if it is just a little bit at a time.

Transforming your attitude can also assist you in curbing the negative spiral of your thoughts, thus keeping your depression from gaining a deeper foothold. Part of the reason that attitude is so critical is based on biology.

Every time you feel bad physically, it only compounds the negative feelings you are dealing with mentally and emotionally.

Changing your attitude is not easy but can be done every time you make a small shift in your thoughts. Over time, these small steps can develop into a big attitude change.

With that in mind, let us discuss a critical way to shift your thoughts and attitude on a daily basis for a profound impact:

1. Healthier lifestyle:
   - Eating/diet
   - Exercising
   - Sleeping routine
   - Socialising

2. Relationships with:
   - Yourself
   - Family
   - Partner
   - Work
   - Children
   - Friends

3. Stress management:
   - Watching your favourite film
   - Reading a good book
   - Practising a hobby
   - Listening to music
   - Writing in a journal
   - Something that help will you to unwind

Your attitude towards your condition is what will help you through those difficult times when you feel like giving up, and can also be a tipping point for you to fight back. It is your attitude that will assist with the changes you have to make in your daily routine, as depression can leave you feeling fatigued, negative, demotivated, and not your usual self.

One daily routine which I incorporated that helped me to combat the lies of depression, those negative statements running through my head about myself, was affirmations.

AFFIRMATIONS

'Affirmation', according to the Collins Dictionary, is "an act of affirming or a state of being affirmed; a statement of the existence or truth of something." Note the word truth here, because that is exactly the point that I am making to you in writing this book. Affirmations are a self-help strategy, used to promote self-confidence and instil belief in your own abilities.

THE QUESTION IS HOW?

Affirmation works by helping to create changes in the brain. Affirmations focused on positive experiences, or core values, can activate the brain's reward systems, potentially making it easier to adopt a more positive outlook towards the future. This works because of another important brain characteristic–neuroplasticity. There are many conversations we can have with others, and more importantly, with ourselves, but the danger to look out for in these conversations is the big lie and in order to counteract that, you have to allow yourself to hear the truth.

This is where affirmations come in, as you go through each day, you will have ceaseless conversations with yourself. You talk to yourself about everything, what is currently happening or what you believe is going to happen. You make assumptions about what someone thinks, or is going to say, formulating ideas about what is in the head of others. You decide what gets fixed or remains broken. Your inner conversation speaks so much louder than you may realise, and is not mere thoughts rolling around in your head, but a voice that speaks both negatively and positively. It is a relationship that you have with yourself, which helps to influence the decisions you make on a daily basis. The conversation you have with yourself can also determine the quality of life that you choose to live. How you talk to yourself decides how you feel about yourself. Depression is a serious disorder; its symptoms of sadness and isolation can be debilitating. You have to do what you can on your own to help yourself treat depression and alleviate its symptoms.

When I think about affirmations, it brings to mind a quote by Ferdinand Foch, "The most powerful weapon on earth is the human soul on fire." This is how I see affirmations. It is like repeatedly chanting something to yourself to keep your soul moving on. When you are in a depressive state, you have filled your mind with negative thoughts, and to change that state, you must fill your mind with positives. It is like having a glass of dirty water. You want a clean glass of water to drink and, to make that possible, something has to happen. In order for you to truly have a clean glass of water, it takes more than emptying the glass and pouring fresh water in. You will also have to wash the glass out because, if you don't, then the dirt will still affect the fresh water. Therefore, you must tackle the symptoms of depression, but you also have to go through the route of your mind.

Every day, our brains are constantly in motion. Not only is our brain handling a multitude of physical things related to the functioning of our bodies, it is also filtering the information we are receiving from the world around us, through our five senses. This filtering process helps us to form our viewpoint and attitude of the people and world around us.

Internally, we have our inner dialogue, the things that we tell ourselves. That inner voice is powerful, and it can end up shifting our thinking in a positive way or turning our thoughts to negative. Affirmations are a way to train our inner voice to steer clear of the negative and focus instead on the positive. For those suffering with depression, this can be a challenge. Our thoughts are spiraling so deeply into negativity that our inner voice cannot allow a positive thought into the mix.

Your inner voice can be used to inspire you, to lift you up, and to motivate you to move from point A to point B. For instance, if your inner voice is telling you that your situation is hopeless, then that is how you will behave, and your actions will reinforce those thoughts. However, you can use your inner voice to concentrate on the positive and good aspects of your life as well.

For example, start the day by focusing on one thing that will go well. Just one thing. Tell yourself repeatedly that it will go right. Let your inner voice motivate you in this one small area. Your mind, particularly your subconscious, will focus on finding things that support what your inner voice is saying. When this happens, you will feel a jolt of happy hormones. This positive experience will encourage you to try more affirmations, which can help you to shift your thinking, one thought at a time. Affirmations are not a cure-all to depression, but they can assist you in pulling your thoughts out of a dark place and back into the light. Transforming your mindset, can help you to feel better. Using your thoughts to change your actions is something that can really help you to see life differently.

Once you reach this point, it can help motivate you to change. You may have heard of individuals using affirmations to keep themselves focused on their aspirations. Depression can take away your desire to set any goals or to reach for them. Affirmations are meant to put your mind back into the mode of setting targets and seeing that it is possible to create change.

It is not easy to shift your thoughts, especially if you have been trapped in a negative spiral for a significant period of time. By using affirmations, you tap into the power of your mind in a meaningful way, because they help you to align your thoughts with your actions and move you towards a goal.

Earlier in this chapter, I spoke about how important it is to acknowledge your depression and where you are struggling in your life.

Once you do so, you will discover areas where your actions and thoughts can be aligned. If you shift your thoughts with the use of affirmations, then you can begin to alter your actions as well. Many of the individuals I work with start by telling themselves something as simple as, "It is going to be a great day." Then, they work on finding ways to make the day great. They become so focused on fulfilling this thought, that they miss all the ways in which the day did not go as well, or they don't stop to dwell on these aspects.

It is possible to have a bad experience during one part of the day and allow it to consume your thoughts, to the point that it negatively impacts everything else. You miss all the wonderful aspects of the day because your inner voice is consumed with what went wrong. Depression amplifies that negativity. Affirmations are meant to break that cycle, help you to readjust, and see past the bad moments. You are reclaiming your power to find joy and happiness by doing so. What types of affirmations can you start with? It can be anything, but I want you to make sure that you say your affirmations in the morning, even before you get out of bed. Then, make a conscious decision to repeat your affirmations throughout the day. It might even help to write your affirmations down and display them in your bathroom, kitchen, or office. Anywhere that you go regularly. Make those affirmations a part of your visual, as well as mental, landscape.

Now let's talk about some of the ways in which you can support your affirmations and encourage yourself on this journey.

I will share a few tips which have helped me with my affirmations, and still help me to this very day:

- Affirmations should be positively stated: they need reinforcement to gain influence.

- They need to relate creating your own affirmations can help to ensure that you are choosing those which will help you the most.

- Keep it real: remember that you are counteracting the negative. Replace depression's lies with the truth.

- Affirmations should be stated in the present: "I will be," "I am."

- Be consistent: affirmations have become a daily habit for me. They are not only important for changing your state of mind once, but also for continuously keeping it in the right state. Consistency eats intensity for breakfast, anytime, any day, anywhere.–Take action: affirmations can help to boost your motivation and confidence, but you still have to encourage yourself to take action and keep at it. Try thinking of affirmations as a step towards change, and not the change itself. That being said, also be patient with yourself.

Changing your mindset is not going to happen in a day, or even a week, but as you introduce affirmations into your routine, the change will begin to happen.

APPLY

When suffering from depression, everything feels too difficult. You feel so low that everything you once knew and used to enjoy seems to fade into darkness. The effort to complete even the smallest task seems overwhelming, whilst the ability to do anything bigger is even harder. I have had moments when the words 'action taker' were painful to hear, and as a man, I felt very depleted, as I should be strong and an 'action taker.' This idea, as well as my cultural beliefs, made me think that I should not have been feeling that way. The fact is that depression does not differentiate between gender, culture or age. It does not matter who you are when the low moments and the darkness hit. It is exceedingly difficult to see light at the end of the tunnel at those times of inertia. It is easy to become discouraged and feel powerless, which perpetuates depression.

You have to fight back. I dread to wonder where I would be now if I had not, if I had submitted to what was happening to me without taking action. You have to come up with a plan to act, the sort that propels you ahead, even when you'd rather lag behind. There is nothing wrong if you cannot do it on your own. GET HELP and do not be ashamed; there is nothing to be ashamed about. Seeking help is so crucial, even though you may be telling yourself that you don't need it. Depression drains your energy, hope, and drive, making it difficult to take the steps that will help you to feel better.

Sometimes, simply thinking about the things you should do to feel better, like exercising or spending time with friends, can seem exhausting or impossible to put into practice. Having that extra hand to give you a little boost or accountability can work wonders. It may not be great at first, as you may feel like lashing out at whoever is helping you. That is totally understandable. Hence, it is especially important that you find someone who has a clear picture of how you are feeling and what you are going through. Please don't assume they know, because trust me, unless they have walked the journey, they have no clue.

Seeking support plays an essential role in overcoming depression. On your own, it can be difficult to maintain a healthy perspective and sustain the effort required to recover. At the same time, the very nature of depression makes it difficult to reach out for help. When you are depressed, the tendency is to withdraw and isolate yourself, so that even connecting to close family members and friends can be tough.

It is crucial that you take one step at a time. Rushing, or pushing yourself too much, can make you become weary and frustrated when things don't go your way, sending you crashing again. It is better to take your time and get it right, rather than rushing to take one step forward, but twenty back. Of course, even when you go slowly you may end up hitting a crash point, but be patient with yourself. The fact that you are taking action at all is a major achievement.

You will not know which of the various strategies or coping mechanisms will help until you try. I once heard an analogy used by my publisher, Michelle Watson, "Having information, but not using it, is like walking and bumping your way through the dark, whilst carrying a flashlight in your hand that you refuse to turn on."

I want to be very honest with you right now. The one person that can help you is YOU, no matter what anyone says or does, the final work is down to you.

ASCERTAIN

There were many things I learned about depression, as I dealt with it during the grieving process following the death of my father. My medical training also helped me to understand how mindset impacts the physical body. Many symptoms of depression can be described in sentences that begin with, "I feel…" Why is knowing this so important?

All of our feelings can be tied to a thought that we have had in the past, or are having right now. Our minds are powerful. Our thoughts affect our decision-making, actions, emotional state, and even our physical well-being. Depression tends to turn our thoughts down a dark path of negativity. Once that negativity takes root, it can become a vicious cycle.

If our thoughts are negative and assume that something will not work, then our brain will focus on making decisions and taking actions that will support the outcome which our negativity creates. Thus, the outcome reinforces the thoughts, and the cycle continues. Ultimately, our minds are designed to stop us from doing anything that might hurt us. Take action and stop waiting. The choice is between the pain of growth or the pain of staying where we are.

Too often, individuals with depression do not recognise the power of their own thoughts. They are too busy making up reasons for why they feel this way, or blaming others. However, as their thoughts continue in that negative spiral, depression only worsens.

When I came up with my five Cs, for the titles of chapters two to six in this book, I recognised how they each play a part in addressing depression and are part of the tools you need to effectively manage it: Cognition, Connection, Communication, Constitution, and Career. There is no magic solution, but depression does not have to rule your life to the point that you can find no joy or happiness.

I believe that knowledge is the power to take our lives in a new direction, or deal with the challenges we face. When we arm ourselves with knowledge and tools, then we give ourselves the power to effect meaningful change in our lives.

While you can opt to work on one of these five areas specifically, to effectively address your depression, you will need to work on all five Cs. I would suggest that you begin by focusing on cognition, as improving your mindset will help you to take further steps.

> **"When you change the way you look at things, the things you look at change."**
> – Dr. Wayne Dyer

3

CONNECTION

RELATIONSHIPS AT THEIR BEST

"The best and most beautiful things in the world cannot be seen or even touched. They must be felt with the heart."
– Helen Keller

One of the most challenging aspects of depression is how isolated and alone many of us feel. It is as if there is a wall between you and the rest of the world. Many of us spend time alone as we deal with depression, and our thoughts continue to feed us a negative narrative that plays over and over because we are not around others who can break through to us.

During my own journey with depression, I saw the importance of relationships and how critical they were to my well-being. Depression lies to us because it tells us that we do not deserve these important relationships and that we are all alone. It tricks us into neglecting the important relationships we have with family and friends.

The loss of my father meant I had to find a new way to connect with my mother, which was not easy, because my father had played such a pivotal role in our interactions. The fact that my mother and I were grieving the loss of someone we loved very much added its own woes. How could I build a better connection with my mother on my own? I felt as if I were now fighting multiple battles, and the one person who could help me was gone. I felt like a stranger to my mother, now more than ever, and not because of anything she did, but because the absence of my dad left a void, a big empty space where the bridge that kept us together once was. I was mourning not only the loss of my dad, but also the loss of my identity.

When we talk about relationships, the first thing that comes to mind is a partner or spouse, but what about the relationship with family or friends? These relationships are also important and crucial on the journey to overcoming depression and its many lies. A solid support network is necessary and will make a massive difference. This was something that, luckily, I realised early, and even though I missed my dad, I felt the need to be closer to my mother than ever before. It was not as easy as I would have hoped, as I was no longer the bubbly, talkative Ikhenemoh, but someone who could not find the energy to talk or express my emotions, especially not to my mother. I needed to fulfill the financial role, give the support that my father once gave, and summon the strength that he represented. But I was drowning, looking for someone to save me instead of being the one who saves others. I felt like an absolute failure, a worthless fraud and a disappointment to my father.

I want to share the relationship elevator roadmap, which incorporates the five As that have helped me on my walk with depression. These are Assessment, Appraisal, Advantage, Assurance, and Approach. Now let's go through each one of these steps and see how they can benefit your relationships and strengthen your social ties. Depression lies and tells us that people do not value their relationships with us. By going through the relationship elevator, you will realise that this is simply another lie and recognise the steps needed to break through it.

RELATIONSHIP ASSESSMENT

The assessment stage involves analysing the state of a relationship. Is it currently the way that you want it to be or do you want to take it to a higher level? If so, what do you need from the relationship and what do you need to put into it?

You need to be honest with yourself and understand where the relationship is right now and the part that you played in getting it to this point. Perhaps you did not open up, or you made assumptions about the individual which had a negative impact. With my mother, I realised that our relationship was just so-so. It was not that we did not talk, but our conversations were somewhat shallow, covering only the basics.

To change that, I had to be willing to open up and show her a different side of who I was. Once she saw that, she would have the opportunity to respond, one way or another. Being open to working on this relationship, instead of throwing my hands up in the air and giving up, meant that I was able to alter my thinking about my mother. It also helped me to break a negative thought process that I did not realise was going in my own head.

Perhaps, as you start to assess the various relationships in your own life, you might recognise a few negative patterns in how you relate to others. Are you focusing solely on the qualities of the person that you do not like, or find irritating?

Part of assessing any relationship is recognising the part that you have played in bringing the relationship to this point.

Here are some other ways to assess a relationship, primarily focused on how you feel about putting energy into it. Some of us need to ask ourselves, "How do I feel about the relationship? Is worth trying to make it better? Is it already a good relationship and one that I want to maintain? Or is it a relationship that is already struggling and I really do not care to make any effort to improve it?

After my father's passing, the first phone call that I had with my mother, she told me, "All is well." I could not help but think, *if this woman who just lost her husband of 50 years could say all is well, then who was I to be depressed?* I also saw this as an opening, a chance to make a change in our relationship. My mother helped me gain some perspective about my situation and my loss. I started to recognise that it was not going to be easy for me to step in and care for this family. I needed to be honest with her about what I was capable of and what responsibilities might need to be shared with others.

Depression places you into a negative frame of mind, making you easily vulnerable to focusing on the negative aspects of your relationships, pointing out ways in which they do not meet your expectations. Remember, the key to any relationship is how well you communicate with each other, outlining what you expect from yourself and what you expect from others. If you have not clearly communicated your expectations, then how can you expect others to meet them? Instead, you build resentment and negativity that feed off each other.

Relationships suffer because of this negative mindset: the reality is that they may actually be suffering from a lack of communication. This stage of assessment is critical to determining how your thinking and communication could be negatively impacting your relationships. Accept that your relationships will not improve if you go into them with the mindset that you are going to change someone else, or fix them. Blaming the other person alone, and focusing on what they need to do to improve the relationship, means you are not taking responsibility for the part that you have played in bringing the relationship to this point.

Instead, focus on what you can change within yourself. What do you expect from yourself? When you start working to meet your own expectations, then your actions and communication skills will change and that will positively impact those relationships. People respond to you based on what you say and do. As you make changes, you will elicit a different response from others. The expectations you have for yourself are different from those you have for others. You need to separate the two first, before you can make any real changes.

A problem with depression is that you feel unhappy with yourself, but see yourself as powerless to change anything. Clearly, this is another lie that depression tells us. If you want to improve any relationship in your life, regardless of who it is with, then you have to do something about how you feel about yourself.

You must accept that you are going to do something about how you feel and set new expectations for yourself, otherwise you will end up losing the people you care about most in your life. We are social creatures, and we cannot thrive without these relationships in our lives. Driving people away because we are unhappy with ourselves does not benefit us, but it feeds into the lies that depression is telling us about ourselves and our value to others. It is particularly important that you take time to assess where you are, as this will help you to figure out where it is that you desire to be, and how to arrive there. I often hear people say 'think outside the box' and I used to wonder how or why that statement makes any sense. However, when I was in a deep state of depression that is exactly how I felt, like I was in a box on my own and no one could possibly understand. Being inside this box throws you into a state of self-pity and self-destruction, you become your own enemy. I was not able to honestly assess my situation or state. I kept telling myself that I was fine until I was honest with myself.

APPRAISAL OF YOUR MINDSET

It all starts with your mindset.

Are you going to change your mindset for the better or continue to live with the worst?

Throughout this journey to uncover the lies of depression, I have focused on your mindset, as well as recognising your ability to take action. Although depression would have you believe that you are a victim, the truth is that you are not powerless. You can take steps to improve your mindset and break through your depression, regardless of the initial trigger.

When it comes to relationships, as part of your assessment, you likely acknowledged some aspects that might need to be fixed or those relationships that are unhealthy. Perhaps you are thinking, "That relationship is not worth saving. I am going to get rid of that person." The problem with ending relationships whilst tackling depression is that you are eliminating people from your life who can support you and help you shift your mindset.

It is worth taking the time to try and repair those relationships, instead of quickly deciding they do not merit the effort. Plus, you are giving others, including those close to you, a chance to understand your brain and what depression is like for you. For example, after spilling water on the kitchen floor, someone with a normal brain (and not dealing with depression) would tell themselves that water was spilt and that they need to take a towel or something and use it to clean up the water. The depressed person would see that same water on the floor and wonder what they are going to do. The water could end up sitting there for a long time because their brain struggles to make the connection between what has happened and what they need to do to address the problem.

When you are depressed, you may feel as if you do not know what to do to fix a relationship, that it is easier to abandon it. I encourage individuals to seek ways to break that cycle of being stuck, wondering what to do. As your mindset shifts because you are taking action, then your brain will begin to make that leap without a conscious effort. This course of action works from both sides.

If you have a loved one dealing with depression, it is important to ask yourself what you can do to help them. For instance, if your outgoing partner becomes depressed and introverted, then your focus should be on the actions you can take to help them become outgoing again. It may be small steps, but with your support, they can overcome the challenges of depression to reclaim the parts of their personality suppressed by depression's lies.

There is always a way out, but you cannot do this on your own without reaching out to others. The situation may not be good right now. Yet, you have the power to decide that you will not let the current situation impact or ruin your relationships. Instead, banding together can be the key to getting through and out to the other side.

Part of what I want to stress here is the importance of reaching out to others, whether you are suffering from depression or have a loved one suffering from it. In either case, taking advantage of any opportunity to connect is critical to breaking through depression and maintaining the most important relationships in your life. In some cases, it can also be the key to even improving your relationships because you are more intentional about your mindset.

PROVIDING ASSURANCE AND ALTERING YOUR APPROACH

The challenging aspects of depression can leave you feeling as if your relationships cannot improve, and nothing will get better. The lie that depression tells us is that if a relationship is suffering, then it cannot be improved and that it will continue to worsen. Providing assurance to your loved ones in this context is about helping yourself, and others, to recognise that today might be bad, and your relationships might be going through a bad time, but tomorrow can be better. For example, with my mother, I understood that depression and grief were making it challenging for both of us, but I was determined to not let it ruin our relationship. Instead, I focused on reassuring myself that it was possible for our relationship to flourish.

It comes back to mindset and trying to determine what you can do to help the other person feel a little bit better. Along with that, you may need to change your approach towards that person. Perhaps you may have to be a bit more tender than usual. Find ways to soften your approach.

Again, it comes back to your mindset. As someone who has dealt with depression, I know that I have to be kind and gentle with myself as I work to change my thoughts and move through depressive episodes. In my other relationships, I have come to realise that if I need to be gentle with myself, then I also need to be gentle with others.

For instance, if your boyfriend or girlfriend is wanting to sleep all day, then yelling at them to get up is not going to be effective. Instead, you have to be gentle, take a softer attitude. It takes a lot of love, care, and patience. Yet, every time a step forward is made, then the lies of depression are exposed by the truth.

Another point is that your approach must include assurance of your love and proof that you care for them. Remember that depression tells us the lies that we are not valuable, or that others do not want to invest in a relationship with us. If you are depressed, do not jump quickly to judge other people's actions, and this applies to those who have someone close to them who is suffering from depression. Assuming the worst of everyone is part of the lies that depression tells us and your approach needs to reflect that you see the best in them, instead of the worst.

Your approach is also wrapped up in your determination to maintain your relationship. This is not always easy, especially when depression often seems to isolate you or your loved ones. Reaching out to connect can be difficult, but it is not impossible. With my mother, my earliest calls were focused on making sure that she was alright and to assess how she was handling her new circumstances without my father.

However, as time went on, we started talking about other things related to her life and mine. Our conversations allowed us to connect on a deeper level and it was very encouraging to me. It demonstrated that a better relationship was possible.

If you are dealing with depression, recognise that the effort which you make to maintain or build up a relationship is worth the time and effort. More often than not, those relationships are meaningful ones to you personally and they will improve in time. The way we communicate with each other is a crucial part of the growth or improvement of any relationship. Too often, depression robs us of the ability to articulate what is going on inside and gives us a viewpoint that is often unrealistic or which makes us quick to assume the worst motives and intentions of others. In the next chapter, I dive into communication and the changes you can make regarding the way that you communicate to benefit yourself and others.

WHAT IS YOUR ADVANTAGE POINT?

What do you have to offer?

For any relationship to work it takes two to tango. There must be a level of understanding between the parties involved, no matter what type of relationship it is. Feelings, communication, respect, they all must be reciprocal in order for you to have and maintain.

In any type of relationship there is always something that you bring, even though you may not know what it is yourself. There is always a factor of dependency and interdependency. What you bring into a relationship is what I have come to label as your advantage point. Personally, knowing this has really helped me. When you are battling depression, you forget what you (initially) brought into a relationship, be it your talent for humour or making jokes, picking other people's brains, making them feel better about themselves. or helping with chores at home. You may be thinking, I cannot even care for myself, where can I find the energy to care about others? You see, changing your mind is changing your relationship. You may also be thinking that what you feel is wrong or missing within a relationship is an indication that something is amiss within you, and you may be asking yourself what lessons you can learn from this. Be mindful that what *you* say means something, what *they* say means everything.

You may want to ask yourself, what has helped me in this relationship in the past? Take note that what you have done until now has built your relationship. Yes, this is your advantage point. Could it be that you enjoyed reading a book to your partner, spouse or kids, and they enjoyed listening? What joy did it bring you when you experienced them listening to you? Could it be cooking a meal for friends? Helping a neighbour by taking her dog out?

Now, I hear that inner voice saying… I am not in a state to do that anymore. That was then, I was happy and feeling well. A better question to ask yourself is, *do I want to feel happy again?* Remember, you are treated the way you teach people to treat you. You have still as much to give, learn and teach even in a depressive state of mind. When you understand and behave with the realisation that in a depressive state of mind you still have enough to offer, this will go a long way to boost your self-esteem. There is no better way to escape negative mind thoughts, whilst you are in a depressive state of mind, than by boosting your self-esteem. Use your built-up assets to be an advantage. Often, what you see in others is usually a reflection of some aspect of you. When you realise that there is nothing lacking in you, but all you desire is to give and share, you stand stronger in a relationship and the whole world belongs to you.

Being in a relationship and having depression can be a challenge. There may be good days and bad, so you are never quite sure what to expect. Think about this also, that the individual you have this relationship with, be it a spouse, partner or any type of relationship, is most probably in a constant mode of wondering what best to do for you, or trying to work out what you want, such as whether you want to stay home or go out, and there may be days where they find you irritable and angry for no apparent reason at all. This can be frustrating for you, but it's also frustrating for them.

If you are depressed then your relationship can become depressed too, and it is especially important that you recognise and remember this. Many people tend to overlook the serious damage that depression creates in relationships. Depression can wreak havoc on your ability to communicate – something I will be speaking about in the next chapter – and your ability to experience and maintain intimacy. Depression can elicit feelings of worthlessness, affecting both your thoughts and behaviour, so as well as it being a nightmare for you, your loved ones also see you change, which equally becomes a nightmare for them as they will struggle and go through the pain of not being able to help you, or know what to do.

You need to maintain your relationships as best as you can, and I know it may feel like you have lost control of everything, including a grip on your emotions, but you need as much support as you can get. Pushing loved ones away is not the way to go.

Yes, you are trying to figure everything out for yourself and don't know what to do, but they can only assist you if you let them know where you are at, the things which you are finding difficult and how best they can help you. This will help them to help you, and be seen less as an irritation, as they will keep trying to make you feel better. Some of what they are trying may actually be triggers for you, but if you don't tell them, you will both be in the dark.

COMMUNICATION 4

WHAT ARE YOU SAYING?

"If you talk to a man in a language he understands, that goes to his head.
If you talk to him in his language, that goes to his heart."
– Nelson Mandela

Sadly, in society there are too many misconceptions about poor mental health, what it means and how people think about someone affected with it. The last thing that someone depressed needs is to be judged negatively. However, opening up about your depression is one of the most effective ways to get the help and support you need at a time when you likely feel vulnerable and alone, especially if you choose to disclose your illness to people that you know and trust.

At times, it is hardest to communicate how you are feeling with your nearest and dearest, causing you to go with the easiest option, which is to remain silent. Depression can drain your energy levels to the point where you feel too tired to talk or even be around anyone. It can also leave you thinking that you are undeserving of anything good, including a relationship. These feelings may be causing you to withdraw, but any distance between you and your partner, or other family members and friends, can leave you feeling worse. I understand that the idea of being open and honest about your depression may be uncomfortable, but it is an incredibly helpful conversation to have, as I have stated previously. When you feel ready, think about how you want to talk to your loved one. Would you feel more comfortable sitting down and having a conversation face-to-face, talking when you are on the go together, or when you're both on the sofa watching a movie? Perhaps you may wish to write some ideas down first.

During your talk, let them know about your symptoms. Try to describe the thoughts and sensations that you experience, as well as the behaviour that they may notice, such as struggling to get out of bed, distancing yourself or seeming quiet in conversations.

SPEAK OUT

The best advice I could give you is not to suffer in silence, even though this is what the lies of depression will have you do. These lies will create numerous scenarios in your head of what could go wrong, or the reaction you may receive if you speak out. The fear of the unknown will keep you from opening up to the people who actually care about you. If you are considering disclosing your diagnosis to the people close to you, but are not sure how to start the conversation, here is something for you to consider - letting other people know about your depression helps to provide a support network for you, especially if your condition worsens, or if you need further assistance. The key is that you do not attempt to deal with depression alone, and the only way that this is possible is if you communicate how you are feeling and speak out. "The opposite of depression is expression," so express thyself to heal thyself.

Our words have power and the way we speak to ourselves creates a big impact on our lives and reflects our self-value. When you show kindness to yourself, you feel happier, which facilitates a speedier recovery. Oliver Wendell Holmes observed correctly when he said, "Language is the blood of the soul into which thoughts run and out of which they grow."

It is a known fact that not many understand depression, or how to relate to or interact with someone trapped in that dark prison. For this reason, you need to be aware that not everyone will understand what you are going through, so carefully choosing whom you confide in, and when, is very important. You may be thinking, "Who should I speak to first?" or, "How many people around me do I need to tell?" Some choose to tell only one person, and others benefit from telling many people in their life. The truth is, you are the expert on your situation and can decide what is best for you.

When it came to speaking out, there are a few pointers that my clients have found to be helpful.

- Try not to worry about what the person will think of your situation: you can only control your thoughts and not someone else's. Also remind yourself that the person you have chosen to speak out to loves you and wants to support you, even if they do not know how.

- Do not assume that because you have spoken out, they know how they can help. Let them know in what way they can assist you and think about what you might like from your friend. Maybe you simply need them to be there for you, or maybe you would just like them to be a listening ear. You may also want to ask them to hold you accountable for any actions that may harm you, like drinking, self-harming etc.

- Remember that their response or reaction is not a reflection on you. It's also not your fault if they're not supportive or lack understanding. If they try to discredit you, gently remind them that you are the one living with depression.
- Set some boundaries, if needed. In other words, if your friend wants to 'fix' the situation, or tries to become your therapist, explain that what you need most from them is their support and encouragement.
- Congratulate yourself on having the courage to share your diagnosis with another person. You have just taken another step forward in your recovery and healing.

LISTEN

Who or what are you listening to?

There is a continuous dialogue in our brains and in our minds. Every microsecond is filled with a thought, even while we sleep. These thoughts are the results of internal conversations you have with yourself. These thoughts are particularly present during silent moments. Who and what you listen to shapes the course of your depression. Who you listen to gives you ideas. These ideas are like water being given to a plant. You are the plant and the idea is the water. But too much water may kill the plant, and too little is also not ideal.

YOUR INTERNAL DIALOGUE

How do you speak to yourself?

In his monumental book, Think and Grow Rich, Napoleon Hill introduced the concept of a mastermind group, in which individuals collectively come together to discuss issues and help one another grow. Napoleon Hill created an internal, imaginary mastermind group of men and women, including both living and non-living individuals, with whom he consulted when he was faced with challenges. He imagined them having discussions with each other. If Napoleon Hill could create his mastermind group, you can do this too. I call it your 'mental board of directors.' Despite all the good intentions of your loved ones and people around you, it may be challenging to openly ask for help. Creating your own private mental board of directors is an indirect way of seeking help without the burden of shame, or any internal objections which you may impose on yourself.

In your mental board of directors, you can include whoever you want. These persons may still be living or might have passed away. You could add people in your immediate surroundings. The people you choose do not need to know about it. You are the chairman or chairwoman of your board of directors. You will observe and depending on your needs, the composition of your mental board of directors will change. I have some outstanding individuals in my mental board of directors: Dr Wayne Dyer, Abraham Lincoln, Thomas Jefferson, and the fictional character, Winnie the Pooh. I fall back to what to Winnie the Pooh famously proclaimed: "You are braver than you believe, stronger than you seem, and smarter than you think."

I began listening regularly to Dr Wayne Dyer soon after my father passed away. I have even come to adopt him as a father. I was introduced to his teaching by my friend, Susanne, who I can never thank enough for casually introducing this man to me. In his book, Your Erroneous Zones, Dyer observes that "If you change the way you look at things, the things you look at change."

When faced with hard and terrifying thoughts, I would find myself asking what 'Abe' (Abraham Lincoln) would do. What would Abe say? Abraham Lincoln, the 16th President of the United States, was a man who experienced personal misery himself and still went on to be one of the greatest presidents. Lincoln was just nine when his mother suddenly died. By the time he was twenty, he also had a buried aunt, sister, and a newborn brother. He didn't have a good relationship with his father. In his book, Lincoln's Melancholy: How Depression Challenged a President and Fueled His Greatness, Joshua Wolf Shenk notes that Lincoln was in his mid-twenties when he had his first breakdown after his fiancée, Ann Rutledge, died. Soon after their engagement, Ann became severely sick and died of a fever of unknown origin. Lincoln suffered what we today would call unipolar depression. He later met Mary Todd and the couple decided to get married on 4 November 1842, in the Springfield mansion of Mary's sister. Three of the four boys born to the Lincolns died before they were nineteen years old; both parents experienced depression following these devastating losses. Only their first child, Robert, lived to adulthood.

Here is an observation from Lincoln regarding grief, bereavement and depression: "*In this sad world of ours, sorrow comes to all, and it often comes with bitter agony. Perfect relief is not possible, except with time. You cannot now believe that you will ever feel better. But this is not true. You are sure to be happy again. Knowing this, truly believing it, will make you less miserable now. I have had enough experience to make this statement.*"

Therefore, I hope you can see why I have someone like this on my mental board of directors. I talk to Abe in trying times. I gather my mental board of directors and allow them to discuss with each other while I actively make notes.

It is important to write down ideas when you capture them in your mind, otherwise, they will disappear. What you write you also become.

How do you choose someone to be in your mental board of directors?

You may ask yourself a couple of questions:

1. Has this person had some similar experience?

2. Despite the good intention, what qualifies him/her to give this advice? In the sales community they call this "qualify hard and close easy." Let the other person save face. Nobody likes to be told what to do, neither do you. It turns out that when you realise that there is nothing lacking in you, but to give and share, you stand stronger in a relationship and the whole world belongs to you.

Sigmund Freud famously said that there two very important things in life, "The sex urge and the desire to be great" and our motives are driven by them. The eminent American psychologist, John Dewey calls it "the desire to be important." Lincoln once wrote, "Everybody likes a compliment." If you want to find the confidence and inspiration that's been missing in your life, you'll want to surround yourself with supportive people. After all, escaping the downside of depression is already enough of a challenge without being surrounded by naysayers and doubters.

> "Show me who your friends are, and I will tell you what you are,"
> – Vladimir Lenin.

In her book, Smart Girls Screw Up Too, Bella Zanesco outlines the type of people and personality types you would like to be with. Zanesco states that when considering whom to include in your inner circle of positivity, there are six helpful personality types to consider:

1. The Catalyst – An eye-opening person who can transform your life by introducing you to exciting ideas and opportunities that likely would have remained hidden otherwise. This may be a creative or well-read friend who is always able to recommend the perfect book to keep you inspired.

2. The Player – The fun-loving friend who refuses to let you indulge in self-pity and always has the kind of smile that reminds you of everything good and beautiful in life.

3. The Nurturer – If you need a shoulder to cry on or someone to bring you chicken soup when you're too sick to get out of bed, the Nurturer is there for you, no questions asked.

4. The Inspirer – A friend who is full of encouragement, wisdom and hope. Whenever you meet up with an Inspirer, you come away brimming with confidence and excitement over life's possibilities.

5. The Challenger – The person to go to when you want to see things in a new light. Challengers get their name because they challenge the status quo. They may not be great at breezy chit-chat, but you value them for their unique perspective and mind-blowing discussions.

6. The Lover – Not necessarily the person you're sleeping with, but rather the person who offers you unconditional love and is always there for a judgement-free heart-to-heart. This person might be a childhood friend or a parent, but no matter what, they're in your corner, even at the worst of times.

There is also a bonus member in your inner circle of positivity:

The Maker – otherwise known as your romantic partner. Later, we'll look at how to find love, but it's important to understand ahead of time that your partner doesn't necessarily have to be all of these other things as well.

Many relationships have failed due to unrealistic demands that a partner be nurturing, inspiring, challenging and playful, along with everything else. Keep in mind that many of these roles are often filled by other people.

In his famous book, The Power of Positive Thinking, Norman Vincent Peale asked the award-winning head of a large, psychiatric hospital, "Why do people become insane?" Behind every level of weakness that you overcome, there is a level of success.

Decide carefully who you listen to, so that you can choose wisely who you will place in your mental board of directors.

OBSERVE

When you are going through depression, you could be dragging your family, friends, or partner down with you. Therefore, I believe it is especially important that both you and those around you remain observant. It is not only crucial to be aware that you are depressed, but also to continue being observant as there will be continuous changes, mood swings and various shifts of emotions that can wreck relationships.

When you are in a relationship and feeling depressed, it is important to understand that it's not only you that suffers. Depression doesn't want you to think about that fact because then you will see that they actually care, instead depression wants you to feel as if you are on your own, that no one understands or wants to help.

Depression makes the non-depressed partner feel helpless and confused as they watch you go through silence or withdrawal. If it is your spouse, they may be experiencing with you the lack of sex, or desire to do anything. As you can imagine, this will worry them. Whilst you are tucked away in your own 'dark place,' they are possibly thinking that this is the turn the relationship is taking and how it is now always going to be. Depression isn't just an occasional sadness. It is a collection of symptoms, including irritability, fatigue, difficulty concentrating, changes in appetite, sleep patterns, feelings of worthlessness or helplessness, a loss of enjoyment in your usual activities, and sometimes suicidal thoughts.

Why am I mentioning all of this? Well, having healthy, open relationships will also help you to get back to your old self, whereas unhealthy relationships will make you struggle and become even more depressed. That is why doing what you can to keep your relationships going will also help you to move in the right direction. Being observant can lead to a greater understanding, which leads to greater and more fulfilling intimacy, which leads to even more understanding, and this is not only from the perspective of an intimate relationship but also with that of those around you. Learning to be highly observant can help in so many ways. The ability to recognise triggers in each other and knowing how to respond effectively in a relationship makes a world of difference.

Observation is not a difficult aspect to implement, you do have to ensure though that you are reading the right signs and not allowing the effects of depression or sentimental thinking to create things that are not there. Practising observance will require all parties involved at times to be an emotional detective: picking up on moods, finding patterns, and really making an effort to understand why a person is behaving the way they are. You, however, as the individual going through depression, shouldn't only see it as something that is impacting you alone, as tempting as that is, but keeping in mind that you are not in this on your own and whatever impacts you will also impact those around you who sincerely care about you.

Through observance it is also worthwhile figuring out the various individuals you need for support in different aspects of your walk with depression. Being able to know who to talk to about specific issues, who to trust or to approach for support is of massive relevance. Being able to have an awareness of your surroundings and those around you is key. You have to know those you can trust because, if you don't, you will then remain silent, keeping things bottled up inside and there is only one word for that – DISASTER!

Observation is a powerful method – use it!

WRITE

Numerous studies have shown that there are powerful benefits of writing as a means for dealing with stress and trauma, as the ability to articulate feelings helps the brain process emotions more effectively. This is where journaling comes in, and may end up being your little safe haven.

Effective journaling leads you on a journey that can help improve your quality of life. This can look different for each person, and the outcomes can vary widely, but they are almost always incredibly positive. Journaling can be effective for many different reasons. It can help to clear your head, make important connections between thoughts, feelings, and behaviour, and even buffer or reduce the effects of your mental illness! In my experience, having an outlet that cannot reply or speak back sometimes helps. Look at it this way, it is better to have a medium to express how you are feeling, rather than holding it all in.

Writing about the thoughts and feelings which arise from your depression is called expressive writing. This will help you to cope with the emotional challenges you go through daily. I am not saying that it is a cure, and it does not necessarily work for everyone, but for me, journaling was amazingly effective and helpful. It gave me time to brain dump, and was my form of letting off steam. I could say how I was feeling without the fear of being judged, and it gave me a chance to read back and reflect. Writing became a source of therapy to me and so many other clients that I have worked with, and I believe that it is worth giving it a try. As the great Paulo Coelho once said, "Tears are words that need to be written."

CONSTITUTION 5

YOUR HEALTH IS YOUR WEALTH

"It is health that is real wealth, and not pieces of gold and silver."
– Mahatma Gandhi

Have you ever stopped and thought about the amount of effort that goes into paying bills, staying in the limelight and setting goals that are for financial gain? This same level of attention is given neither to physical nor emotional health, yet health is the greatest asset one can have. I want you to stop and think about it for a moment: how much can you enjoy if you are sick, unable to move or closed away in one room, where you are only able to look at the four walls, having someone else determine how your day ahead will be? Let me be very blunt and not sugar coat it, as we tend to do to avoid facing the harsh reality. The scary truth is that nothing you own or accumulate in life is valued, unless you are alive. A healthy mind is as important as a healthy body, but sometimes we can forget just how important it is to form habits that ensure that we are happy, confident, and secure. We all understand that we should eat well and get plenty of exercise, but what can we do to make sure that we are emotionally strong, resilient, and content, as well as physically healthy?

HABITS

1.   Do you rest?

Rest is vital, however, this is an area in which I struggled immensely, particularly after my father died. The feeling of now being the one responsible for the family weighed heavily on me, and the lack of rest was a major challenge for me daily. My father's death was merely a single contribution to the other million thoughts which floated around in my mind, especially at night. I found it extremely hard to sleep, or even rest, as I saw this as a sign of being lazy (a common thought in our culture). You also have to remember that rest is not only about sleeping, but taking a break as well, giving yourself some time to unwind from the business of the day. When going through depression many negative thoughts attack the mind, and feeling the need to unwind may add additional pressure.

We spend around a third of our lives in bed, and sleep is equally as vital as eating, drinking, and breathing. Going even a couple of days without a good night's sleep can have a huge impact on your emotions, memory, and critical thinking abilities. A common misunderstanding of people with mental health concerns is that they should simply 'pull themselves together', or 'get up and do something!', but in reality, it's not as easily done. It is more important that these issues are addressed and understood, as they can often be both a contributing factor and a side effect of a mental illness.

Ensure that you have an established sleep schedule and stick to it. Go to bed at a set time, and this means no television or mobile phones! In fact, it's probably best to keep screens out of the room altogether, if possible, and only go to bed when you intend to sleep. Your brain is fantastic at making connections, and it's important that your brain connects your bedroom with sleeping. Make sure the room is comfortable and free of distractions, and if you can't sleep, pick up a book and read for a while rather than scrolling through Facebook!

2. Think positive thoughts!

I wish this were an easy task, but unfortunately it is not. Having the ability to start and go through the day on a positive note is one of the most difficult things for a depressed individual to do. Sometimes, when we feel low, positivity can feel like an impossible task, but there is loads of evidence which says that positive thinking can have a major impact on your mood, making you feel more positive and increasing your mood even further! It is a fantastic, happy cycle, and we should do everything we can to enter it.

Being positive doesn't mean you have to be happy all the time. It means that even on hard days, you know that there are better days coming.

Start small. Every morning, tell yourself out loud that today is going to be a good day. When something good happens, no matter how small, notice it! We are all excellent at remembering the bad and forgetting the good. Try to pay special attention to the good things in your life, even something as small as sharing a smile with a total stranger. Concentrate on those small blessings and remind yourself that they exist.

3.   Exercise and eat well

I struggled for a while to develop a healthy diet as I would either, eat on the go, or venture to the other extreme of wanting to just pull the sheets over my head. If the words 'I will do it tomorrow' resonate, then you know what I am talking about. You may think that this means having to go to the gym and pump heavy weights to exercise, but sometimes something as simple as a quick stroll can make all the difference. I know it sounds cliché, but the saying 'healthy body, healthy mind' is absolutely true! We are biological machines, and if we use the wrong type of fuel, or allow our joints to rust, then everything else will be impacted. You don't need to enter a triathlon, or drink only protein shakes and eat broccoli. You can begin by getting outside and moving around, even if it's only for ten minutes a day. A small amount of exercise and fresh air can have a huge impact. Try to make sure that you eat something green with every meal, avoid junk food, cut down on carbs and sugar, and maybe consider brushing up on your cooking skills. You will be amazed at the difference that these little changes will make to your mood. They are a great opportunity to cleanse your mind and delete those negative thoughts and depressed feelings.

If you are still on the fence about what exercise can do for you, let me fill you in the details:

- Endorphins: physical activity kicks up the endorphin levels, the body's feel-good chemicals which are produced by the brain and spinal cord and create feelings of happiness and euphoria.

- Decreased stress: increasing your heart rate reduces stress-induced brain damage by stimulating the production of neurohormones, like norepinephrine, which not only helps your condition, but also improves thinking clouded by stressful events.

- Increased self-esteem and self-confidence: there is no shortage of physical achievements that come about from regular exercise. All those achievements can add up to a boost of self-esteem and the confidence that comes with it.

- Improved sleep: physical activity increases body temperature, which has calming effects on the mind, leading to less sheep-counting and more shut-eye.

- Brain boost: cardiovascular exercise creates new brain cells, a process called neurogenesis, and improves overall performance. It also prevents cognitive decline and memory loss by strengthening the hippocampus, the part of the brain used for memory and learning.

4. Give yourself a break!

Technology can be a curse as well as a blessing! In this age that we live in, there is so much pressure, and it is a fast-paced world. Social media and the internet mean that we obtain our information quickly and are always on the go, absorbing information and responding emotionally. In some ways, this is great: we are more connected than ever before, we can communicate with friends and family wherever we are, and we have new support networks available to us which we would not have had access to twenty years ago.

But this technology can also cause stress, anxiety, a feeling of being overwhelmed and huge pressure to be always available. The worst part is the pressure to compare your life to others on various social media platforms, who portray their lives to be perfect. We all know that this is not the case, as everyone has one issue or another going on in their lives, some choose to be authentic and real about what goes on, whilst others choose to wear a mask that says 'my life is perfect.'

I advise you to go easy on yourself! Practise some self-care, and make sure you put aside some time for yourself. Go out into nature and spend some time away from your screens. Try to reduce the time you spend on social media, and if you're a news junkie, maybe consider reducing the amount of time you spend reading about current affairs, especially during this time of pandemic. The constant input of bad news will only increase your anxiety level. Feel free to switch off from everything for a while; believe me, you are not missing out on anything that will not still be available later. It is alright to have some downtime and concentrate on things that relax you and make you feel happy, whatever those things may be.

Going outdoors and accessing a daily dose of nature can increase focus as well as enhance creativity, problem solving and critical thinking. Action brings motivation. If getting to nature is difficult for you, you may consider bringing nature into your home, using some of these ideas:

- Put up pictures of natural terrain, such as mountains or forests.

- Before you go to bed, step outside and look at the stars.

- Make your phone/computer screensaver a picture of nature.

- If you have no outside space, consider a window box or house plants.

- Think about adopting a pet, or offer to look after a neighbour's pet.

5.   Pick up a hobby!

If you do not have one, get a hobby. Finding a hobby you love is a fantastic creative outlet! One of the best ways to maintain a healthy mind is to keep your brain active and occupied. If you have a hobby already, try to make sure that you keep it up. One of the first things that we tend to do when we feel low is to stop doing things that previously made us happy, and it is important to avoid this if possible. If you have lost track of your hobbies, do not worry! Try to take some small steps to pick them up again and get back into them. You could even consider something entirely new! This could be anything, from sewing, to fishing, to whistling, to playing a musical instrument; anything that interests you and gives you something to focus on in a positive way. The internet is an incredible resource for picking up information about possible new hobbies that are cheap or free and can be started almost immediately. Some of them may even have local organisations or clubs to attend, which have the added bonus of encouraging you to meet other people with similar interests. Do not worry if this doesn't appeal, there are plenty of hobbies that you can do on your own, if that's more your style.

6.   Be mindful!

Take time to stop and appreciate your surroundings, who you are and what you have, no matter how small. Mindfulness is a technique that teaches you to concentrate on how you are feeling in the moment and pay attention to physical sensations and emotional reactions. Life is all about how you see it. You can choose to look at things from the perspective of the glass being half-empty or half-full. There is a mountain of evidence suggesting that practising mindfulness regularly encourages us to let go of negative encounters from the past and anxieties about the future, and pay attention to our experience of life as it occurs. Focus on the physical sensations, sounds, smells, or tastes of your day-to-day routine. Notice how things make you feel and how your body and mind react to them. Do not try to deny emotions or run away from them, just notice them, understand them, and move on. Do not worry if it doesn't work immediately. Mindfulness is a technique that takes practice and needs time to develop, but if you stick with it, then it will help enormously.

7. Open up!

Sometimes a friendly word from someone you trust can make all the difference. Despite all our best efforts, it can sometimes still feel difficult to be honest about our struggles with mental health. We do not always know how people are going to react, and that can be scary. But being honest with yourself, allowing yourself to be vulnerable, and asking for help is an important part of staying mentally healthy. You are not made of stone, everyone struggles sometimes, and the best thing you can do for yourself, and for everyone else, is to be honest and open. This could be something as small as calling a friend and asking to talk, going online and finding an anonymous support network, if that is easier, or it could be something bigger, like calling a doctor and asking for help, or attending a local support group. Whatever route is best for you, talking to other people and asking for advice, support and guidance can be an incredibly fulfilling experience. Maybe one day you will be the person that someone turns to when they need help or advice, and you'll be able to offer them the same help that you received when you needed it the most.

It can be easy to forget how important it is to look after our mental health, but if you take steps to embed healthy habits now, they will pay off in the future. The steps above are a great place to start!

ADJUST

Based on your diagnosis, you may have to make some reasonable adjustments. Naturally, you may want to shut yourself away from the world and not deal with the situation, but you will have to adapt and adjust as you move on. Treating depression effectively means doing more than taking medication and going to therapy. The more you change your lifestyle to ensure a healthy mind and body, the more you will be able to cope with the challenges of depression. There are six basic things which I believe you need to thrive psychologically:

1. Reciprocal friendship
2. An intimate relationship (I will elaborate more in Chapter Six on intimacy being a basic human need.)
3. A career with future prospects
4. A daily routine
5. A good diet
6. A healthy relationship with prescription drugs

LITTLE STEPS

Taking the first steps is usually the hardest part of the journey. Often, someone is not sure about the best direction to take or what to start implementing. Their dreams and aspirations at this point can seem far away. Therefore, there can be a temptation to wait until the entire road map is available, or else not commence at all. It becomes a waiting game for all the pieces of the puzzle to be available and make sense, for the right conditions and circumstances, whilst a procrastination infestation ensues through overanalysing and saying 'I will do it tomorrow.' The other route you may venture down is not a waiting game, but an actual full stop. Be consistent. You may not feel like it right now, but pushing yourself to take one miniature step a day, or even a week, is better than nothing at all.

TRACK

As you gradually take your steps, you should measure what worked, what did not work and, more importantly, what triggers you negatively. Tracking your progress is an important part of the process, but it can also add to your triggers if you begin to put pressure on yourself, or feel as if you have not made enough improvement. Remember that you are not in a race with anyone. Working at your own pace and praising yourself for even the smallest of achievements will go a mighty long way. Doubt, fear, worry and uncertainty are common factors that stop people from taking action, especially when they are suffering from depression. Thinking that you have to take big steps to start out can become a paralysing thought. Little steps taken over time have the potential to make a difference. Small steps and actions add up incrementally.

Look out for these five points when tracking your progress:

- What worked?
- What did not work?
- What caused you to become overwhelmed?
- What you can implement to make the steps you are taking easier?
- What can you praise yourself for?

HARMONISE

Having a daily routine is key to helping you escape from a constant, downhill, spiraling mood. People who are battling depression tend to think that they are weak, but actually they are very strong. They fight every single day, and wake up each morning knowing that they will have to get up and continue fighting another day.

Give yourself a fighting chance by taking your M.E.D.S.:

Meditation (Mindfulness)

The symptoms of depression can linger, even with treatment. You may have tried many methods which haven't helped as much as you hoped, and you may want to consider adding meditation into the process. Depression can involve a lot of dark thoughts. You might feel hopeless, worthless, or angry at life and even at yourself at times, wanting to stop feeling the way you do. This can make meditation seem somewhat counterintuitive, since it involves increasing awareness around thoughts and experiences. However, meditation enables you to learn how to pay attention to your thoughts and feelings without passing judgment or criticising yourself.

Meditation does not involve pushing away dark thoughts or pretending you don't have them. Instead, you notice and accept them, then let them go. In this way, meditation can help disrupt cycles of negative thinking.

Imagine that you are sharing a peaceful moment with your partner. You feel happy and loved. Then the thought, "They're going to leave me," comes into your mind and that peaceful moment becomes a torment.

Meditation can help you to:

- Notice this thought.
- Accept it as one possibility.
- Acknowledge that it is not the only possibility.

Instead of following this thought with something like, "I'm not worthy of a good relationship," meditation can help to let this thought cross your awareness and keep going. Meditation helps us become more aware of what is happening within. It also allows us to relate more directly – with benevolence – to the emotions which are brought to light, including anger, stress, anxiety, and craving. A study published in the Journal of the American Medical Association (JAMA) in 2014 found that meditation was about as effective as medication in treating depression. This study, which was notable for its scope and rigorous methodology, raised yet another voice in favour of a multi-remedied approach to help alleviate the disorder. As Johns Hopkins University's Dr Madhav Goyal, who led the research team, put it, "Also relevant for physicians and patients is that there is no known major harm from meditating, and meditation doesn't come with any known side effects. One can also practice meditation along with other treatments one is already receiving."

The aim of meditation is not to push aside stress or block out negative thinking, but rather, to notice those thoughts and feelings, all the while understanding that you do not have to act on them. This could be as simple as closing your eyes and repeating a single phrase or word, or counting breaths. Meditation can also help to prepare the brain for stressful situations. For example, meditating for a few moments before a doctor's appointment or social situation can help to shift the brain and body out of stress response and into a state of relative calm.

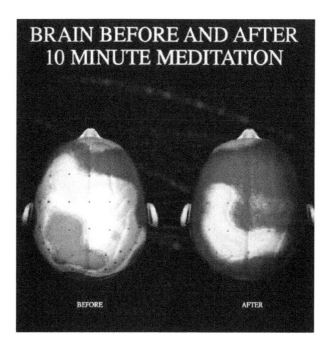

Diagram–brain illustrating effect of meditation/mindfulness before and after meditation.

Exercise

Physical activity, along with food choices and stress levels, can profoundly affect mood and reduce the risks of anxiety and depression. Depression can be exhausting and frustrating, but exercise can really help, more than many realise. Physical activity boosts your mental health and helps to benefit people going through depression and battling the 'blues'. Walking was one of the most effective forms of exercise that worked for me when I was depressed, and even now. I was able to clear my head and enjoy nature, as I paid more attention than I normally would to the trees, the refreshing air, the birds landing for a munch, and even the squirrels rummaging around for something to eat. It gave me the chance to free my mind of the troubling thoughts that would loom in a grey cloud over my head, and allowed me to immerse myself in my environment. Going for a walk can do wonders for one's mental health. It improves self-perception and self-esteem, mood and sleep quality, and it reduces stress, anxiety and fatigue. Daily walking prevents fat deposition and maintains normal blood circulation. Those who do not have time to exercise now will soon find time for illness.

Diet

There is no specific diet to treat depression, but eating more of some foods and less, or none, of others can help some people to manage their symptoms. One factor that may contribute to depression is a person's dietary habits, which will determine the nutrients that they consume.

Incorporating a healthy diet into your routine can help to boost your mood. Here, I list a few nutrients, and the foods in which they can be found, to assist you in getting on the right track.

A. Selenium

Some scientists and trusted sources have suggested that increasing selenium intake might help to improve mood and reduce anxiety, which may make depression more manageable.

Selenium is present in a variety of foods, such as:
- Whole grains
- Brazil nuts
- Some seafood
- Organ meats, such as liver

B. Vitamin D

People obtain most of their vitamin D through sun exposure, but dietary sources are also important.

Foods that can provide vitamin D:
- Oily fish
- Fortified dairy products
- Beef liver
- Egg

C. Omega-3

Eating omega-3 fatty acids may reduce the risk of mood disorders and brain diseases by enhancing brain function and preserving the myelin sheath, which protects nerve cells.

Good sources of omega-3 fatty acids include:

- Cold-water fish, such as salmon, sardines, tuna and mackerel
- Flaxseed, flaxseed oil and chia seeds
- Walnuts

D. Antioxidants

Vitamins A (beta carotene), C, and E contain substances called antioxidants. These help to remove free radicals, which are the waste products of natural bodily processes that can build up in the body. Fresh, plant based foods, such as berries, are good sources of antioxidants. A diet that is rich in fresh fruits and vegetables, soy, and other plant products may help reduce the stress-related symptoms of depression.

E. Vitamins B-12 and B-9 (folate or folic acid)

These sources will help and maintain the nervous system, including the brain. They may assist in reducing the risks and symptoms of mood disorders, such as depression.

Sources of vitamin B-12 include:
- Eggs
- Meat
- Poultry
- Fish
- Oysters
- Milk
- Some fortified cereals

Foods that contain folate include:
- Dark leafy vegetables
- Fruit and fruit juices
- Nuts
- Beans
- Whole grains
- Dairy products
- Meat and poultry
- Seafood
- Eggs

F. Zinc

Zinc helps the body to perceive taste, but it also boosts the immune system and may influence depression. It has been suggested that zinc levels may be lower in people with depression and that zinc supplementation may help antidepressants to work more effectively.

Zinc is present in:
- Whole grains
- Oysters
- Beef, chicken and pork
- Beans
- Nuts and pumpkin seeds

G. Protein

Protein enables the body to grow and repair, but it may also aid people with depression. The body uses a protein called tryptophan to create serotonin, the 'feel-good' hormone.

Tryptophan is present in:
- Tuna
- Turkey
- Chickpeas

SLEEP

People with depression may find it difficult to fall asleep and stay asleep during the night. They can also have excessive daytime sleepiness, or even sleep too much due to fatigue. Understanding the complex relationship between sleep and depression can be an important step in improving sleep quality and better managing mental health. Depression and sleep issues have a bidirectional relationship. This means that poor sleep can contribute to the development of depression, and having depression makes a person more likely to develop sleep issues.

Tips for sleeping:
- Make sure your bedroom is comfortable and not too noisy.
- Try not to work or have your computer or TV in your bedroom.
- Try not to eat or drink too much late at night–have your evening meal earlier if you can.
- Spend some time relaxing before you go to bed – a warm bath may help. There are many different relaxation techniques, such as meditative audio recordings.

- Try to follow a regular sleeping pattern.

- Keep a notepad by your bed, then if you are worried about something, you can write it down and be ready to deal with it the next day.

- Complementary therapies, such as massages or aromatherapy, can be a good way to relax.

Overall, creating a daily routine, or what I call healthy habits, can make a massive difference in your improvement.

What is your daily routine?

If you do not have one, now may be the time to create one. Do not expect to get it right constantly, but remember what I mentioned earlier – all it takes is one small step at a time.

6

CAREER

WHERE DO YOU GO FROM HERE?

"Too much choice is not freedom, it is confusion."
– Anonymous

The relationship between work and depression is one that can go both ways. Depression can impact your ability to perform your job well, whilst stress at work can also contribute to a person becoming depressed. If you suffer from depression, you may sometimes find it tough to perform the tasks you need to do as part of your job. Occasionally, it may even be too difficult to go to work. Do not worry, you are not alone. The Office of National Statistics (ONS) has shown that mental health conditions like depression, anxiety and stress are the third most common reason for people being absent from work.

Some work-related triggers that can cause major stress include:

- A high workload
- Being asked to do things outside your competency level

- Sudden changes or difficulties with colleagues

The symptoms of depression which can affect your ability to work may include:

- Finding it hard to remain motivated
- Struggling to concentrate
- Difficulty sleeping
- Losing interest in activities you previously enjoyed
- Difficulty socialising

When you start to develop symptoms of depression, such as feeling low and anxious, struggling to complete your workload, or not being able to manage normal stresses particularly well, it can be good to talk things through with someone you trust. This may be your spouse, another relative, or a trusted colleague at work. During this time, try to talk about whether it is the job that is possibly causing your symptoms.

If you feel that your work is contributing to you becoming depressed or have anxiety about going back to work, try to address the issues with your line manager. If you feel that your symptoms are not being caused by your job, try to identify what else in your life could be contributing to you feeling depressed and try to address these issues.

It is important to seek help. Visiting your doctor can be a good first step, and where available, occupational health support at your work can also be helpful.

FREQUENTLY ASKED QUESTIONS

There are two important days in a man's life: the day he was born and the day he discovers his purpose. Depression is not one of these days and leaves you at times with some unanswered questions.

The quality of the answers you have is dependent on the quality of the questions you ask. The quality of your life is also dependent on the quality of the answers.

You may want to consider:

- Where do you find yourself right now?

- When you wake up in the morning, how do you feel about your career or going to work, now that you are going through this phase of battling depression?

- In the morning, what mood do you wake up in?

- Do you set yourself up to start work every morning feeling inspired?

- Is it possible that your work contributed somehow to what you are going through now? Could it be that you are not getting fulfilment from your current job?

- Remember, you are not your job.

- Could this be a pivotal moment for career change?. How fulfilling is your job?

- Do you lend your identity to your job? Do you find yourself saying "should", "ought to", "have to"?

- Where do you go from here?

These questions presuppose that life is happening to you and not for you. When I started the changing and reframing the questions I started gaining more clarity. Clarity helps in taking laser-focused action. Reframing is a powerful technique in seeing the questions you ask yourself from a different perspective. Ralph Waldo Emerson reminds us that thoughts are the ancestor of action. When thoughts emerge what questions do you ask yourself? Do you reframe these questions? Responsibility is high value for me. Interestingly, when I started questioning its value to me and asking the wrong question, the weight and burden of responsibility grew on me. When I reframed that by asking myself, "Could this responsibility on my shoulder be a sign of greatness?" the weight and burden on me felt much lighter.

The quality of your questions is directly proportional to the quality of your life and your future. Today, when facing a challenge that carries with it any amount of responsibility, this is what I tell myself. Responsibility is a sign of my greatness. If you are struggling to reframe, please find here some questions you may want to consider:

- Why does it matter what you are doing?
- Why does it matter what you will do?
- Why does it matter if you do it?
- Are you committed to your work or are you just interested?

The quality of the questions you ask yourself also stems from your character and values. Belief is something you hold to be true. Value is that which you find to be important. As you ponder over these questions, remember, depression lies. It convinces you that you have no discernible skills and no worthwhile contribution to give to the world. In research published in the Journal of Affective Disorders, Andrea Zülke and her colleagues in their LIFE study concluded that being out of work can increase a person's overall risk of depression.

If time and money was no issue and you had all the time in the world what would you do?

Would you be doing what you are doing right now?

FITNESS TO SERVE

Have you answered the above two questions? Additionally, ask yourself:

Am I suited to serve and carry?

You may want to answer that question and put it into practice. Not knowing if you are fit is detrimental to your health and the community you are serving. The question that normally sticks out like a sore thumb in the forefront of your mind is, am I using my God-given unique talent?

FREEDOM

In his monumental essay, A Theory of Human Motivation, US psychologist, Abraham Maslow, identified a hierarchy of five levels of human needs:

Basic needs

- Physiological – food, water, sex, sleep, rest
- Safety – security, stability, freedom from fear

Psychological needs

- Social – relationships, love, friends
- Self-esteem – achievement, mastery, significance, respect

Self-fulfilment needs

- Self-actualisation – realising personal potential, self fulfilment, seeking personal growth

There have been many updates to this model. Some even argue that at the very base should be the internet and Wi-Fi connection, my 12 year old nephew would agree. I believe that Maslow provided us with insight into the human psyche and human needs. However, I disagree with the notion you must fulfil one level before you move to the next. The main point of Maslow's model is that it is linear, meaning that, before progressing to the next level, you have to satisfy the previous one. I do not agree that they necessarily have to go in that order.

Jessen Chinnapan, my business coach and author of The Great Business Jailbreak™, Billion Lives Changed™ Facebook group, ex-psychiatric nurse, acclaimed business mentor and multiple international speaker awards winner, observed that the supposed linear growth doesn't serve or aid us anymore. He emphasises the fact that we are living in fast-changing times and you don't have to fulfil one need in Maslow's hierarchy of needs before you move to the next level. Chinnapan expands on this in his yet to be published book, Maslow's Hierarchy of Needs Revisited, and divides human needs into Primal and Evolved.

The primal needs he includes survival, respect, curiousity, intimacy, spirituality and freedom. A lack or deficit of these needs may lead to depression.

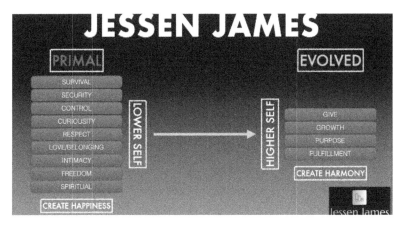

Copyright @Jessen James (permission granted)

Every human has that desire to be free: freedom to achieve a self-actualised self. We have witnessed this during the current global pandemic. Governments told people that they could not leave their house. What did we notice? People felt like they were going crazy with a sense of desperation and in many cases this lead to depression because people felt their freedom was taken away from them.

You may be happy to work for your employer. However, if your job or career gives you certain restrictions you may fall into depression. Imagine for a moment what your life would be like if your vocation was truly your vacation meaning. Now imagine if your vocation stays in the way of achieving this freedom. Remember, you are not your job. Ask yourself, "Did your current job contribute to your fall into depression?" Do not misunderstand, I am not suggesting that you indulge in some juvenile fantasy of not having to work. Imagine feeling inspired and clear about your next career plan, whether that is staying with your present job, considering a new path, or deciding to become an entrepreneur that may provide you with the freedom that you may be lacking.

FINANCES

Your mental health is like money, you don't realise the value of it until you have lost it. If you ask someone who is depressed about the state of their financial situation, this is likely one of the last things they want to talk about. This is understandable, it is that drawer which one doesn't want to open because it is a constant reminder of where one does not want to be. I get that. Anyone who has suffered from depression will tell you that it is debilitating to be unable to stop dwelling on negative thoughts, and the conditions that could have caused them, ie, financial state. Likewise, your health is your wealth. Taking good care of your wealth goes a long way in helping you to take care of your well-being. What is wealth? Let us break the word wealth into 'weal' and 'th'. The word 'wealth' stems from the English word "weal". A common saying is, "money is the root of all evil." I would argue that lack of love is the root of all evil. Self-care is self-love. Self-love also means taking an honest look at your financial situation. Many people live in a fantasy world when it comes to wealth building.

Here are 5 actionable tips you can use to manage your finances better while dealing with depression.

Tips:

1. Avoid overspending while you are feeling unwell
2. Focus on debt reduction
3. Use a savings account
4. Concentrate on recent progress, instead of future challenges
5. Consider debt counselling

Working out your financial habits and thought patterns around money is a good place to begin. It could help you to start to think about the things you want to work on, such as:

When you spend, or save money, and why.

What aspects of dealing with money makes your mental health suffer? Is it attending appointments, opening envelopes, confrontation, or being misunderstood? Or is it something else?

Keep a diary of your spending, and your mood. Try to record what you spent and why. Record how you were feeling before, and afterwards too. This could help you work out any triggers or patterns.

When you understand more about what's happening in your life, you can discover what might help. Sometimes, simply being aware of these patterns can help you feel more in control.

FUTURE

> "Just don't give up trying to do what you really want to do. Where there is love and inspiration, I don't think you can go wrong"
> – Ella Fitzgerald

When each day begins you have a choice. You can ask yourself, what shall I do today? What priority are you giving your life? Do I really want to reclaim my life? My guess is, yes, otherwise you would not be holding this book in your hands or have read this far. What is your purpose for the day?

I hear you say, "Dr Ikhenemoh, that is the point, I do not have a purpose in my life." In reply, let me ask you this, why are you here, on this page of this book? Could it be that it is still worth giving it a 'try'? I usually avoid using the word 'try' as it presupposes that you will not apply your best effort. Birds don't try to fly, they just fly. Looking into the future can seem a daunting task, so let's use what you have. The present is the gift that you have with you right now. Someone once told me that the past is history, the future is a mystery and this moment is a gift, that is why it is called the *present*.

Deepak Chopra makes an interesting observation with The Law of Least Effort in his book the Seven Spiritual Laws of Success. Chopra says that if you embrace the present and become one with it, merge with it, you will experience a fire, a glow and a sparkle of ecstasy throbbing in every sentient being. Only then will you become light-hearted, carefree and joyous.

Mindset is everything. This too shall pass.

8 LITTLE STATEMENTS THAT CAN HELP

It won't last forever – When things are good or bad, remember it will not always be this way. Take one day at a time.

Enjoy every great moment – Your happiness will not come to you, it can only come from you. No one else can make you happy, it's up to you.

Happiness is a choice – This is a profound statement. To be or not to be, happy, or not. Stop waiting for the right person to come into your life, be the right person to come into someone else's life.

Look at depression from different perspectives – Who called it depression by the way? I read the other day that deep rest is probably a better way of describing it – deep rest.

Invest in yourself – You are the most important investment you'll make in your life. Your mental health is more important than your productivity.

Depression may be a blessing in disguise – In my case, as an afterthought, depression has been a blessing in disguise. I do miss my father, oh you bet, every single day, and I know the transformation I have been through would never have happened if I didn't go through the depression.

Even in hell, hope can flower – As Zig Ziglar famously said… "People often say that motivation doesn't last. Well, neither does bathing – that's why we recommend it daily." I am all for positive thinking, but it leads nowhere unless it is followed by positive action.

There is hope – The fact that you are alive means that there is hope for tomorrow. Many others have been where you are, and they have made it by turning depression on its head.

I do not pretend that this book solves all the problems that depression brings. That would be too pretentious of me. But, I do know that you deserve an awesome life. Give yourself a chance to reclaim your life from the clutches and lies that depression tells you. The sad fact is that when you embrace the lies of depression, you stop believing that you deserve a good life worthy of living, and this affects how you see yourself. This is where self-love is essential.

CULTIVATE SELF-LOVE

When self-love is cultivated, the challenging work of changing yourself is softened by the balms of patience and self-compassion. Change is hard enough on its own, especially when you know that you'll inevitably face obstacles along the way on the journey fighting depression. Cultivating a healthy sense of self-love will allow you to be gentle with yourself as you navigate any unavoidable challenges. Knowing that you love yourself unconditionally will anchor you when your journey gets tough. Getting unstuck can be uncomfortable. You might feel vulnerable as you confront the things about yourself that are contributing to the status quo. Change is a process, one which requires you to exercise patience and compassion with yourself. It's okay to be vulnerable; it means you're being honest with yourself. Each change you make moves through a cycle – pre-contemplation, contemplation, preparation, action, and maintenance.

Yes, you can pretend that your life was a masterpiece that you once had or dreamed of. Trying is lying. Stop trying and start doing. Develop the mental range of motion that keeps you free. Imagine you were getting married to your partner, and your partner was you. Would you like to be married to you? Get remarried back to yourself. Make your life a masterpiece. Every choice you make has a price. One choice you can always make is to decide not to change. So, my question is, what do you want? The pain of staying where you are, or the pain of growth. The journey of a thousand minds begins now. Every behaviour satisfies a need. Here is a great reminder from a member from my mental board of directors, Winnie the Pooh: "You are braver than you believe, stronger than you seem, and smarter than you think."

Practising self-love can be difficult for many, especially in times when you face serious challenges. It is not about being self-absorbed or narcissistic, it's about getting in touch with yourself, your well-being and your happiness. You must practise self-love to enable you to push through your limiting beliefs and live a life that truly shines.

The fact that you are alive means that there is hope for tomorrow

Do yourself a favour, take a deep breath, give yourself a little hug and start practising the following:

1. Start each day by telling your self something really positive. How well you handled a situation, how lovely you look today. Anything that will make you smile.

2. Fill your body with food and drink that nourishes it and makes it thrive.

3. Move that gorgeous body of yours every single day and learn to love the skin you're in. You can't hate your way into loving yourself.

4. Don't believe everything you think. There is an inner critic inside of us trying to keep us small and safe. The downside is that this also stops us from living a full life.

5. Surround yourself with people who love and encourage you. Let them remind you just how amazing you are.

6. Stop the comparisons. There is no one on this planet like you, so you cannot fairly compare yourself to someone else. The only person you should compare yourself to, is you.

7. End all toxic relationships, people who make you feel anything less than amazing do not deserve to be a part of your life.

8. Celebrate your wins no matter how big or small. Mentally pat yourself on the back and be proud of what you have achieved.

9. Step outside of your comfort zone and try something new. The feeling we get when we realise we have achieved something we didn't know or think we could do before is incredible.

10. Embrace and love the things that make you different. This is what makes you special.

11. Realise that beauty cannot be defined. It is what you see it as. Don't let any of those Photoshopped magazines make you feel like your body isn't perfect. Even those models don't look like that in real life.

12. Take time out to calm your mind every day. Breathe in and out, clear your mind of your thoughts, and just be.

13. Follow your passion. You know that thing that gets you so excited, but scares you at the same time. The thing that you really want to do, but have convinced yourself it won't work. You should do that!

14. Be patient and persistent. Self-love is ever-evolving. It's something that needs to be practised daily, but can

take a lifetime to master. Be kind and support yourself through the hard times.

15. Be mindful of what you think, feel and want. Live your life in ways that truly reflect this.

16. Treat others with love and respect. It makes us feel better about ourselves when we treat others the way we hope to be treated. That doesn't mean that everybody will always repay the favour, but that's their problem, not yours.

17. Find something to be grateful for every day. It's inevitable that you are going to have your down days. This is fine and very human of you. It's especially important on these days to find at least one thing you are grateful for, as it helps to shift your mind and energy around what's going on.

18. Reach out to family, friends, healers, whomever you need to help you through the tough times. You are not expected to go through these alone.

19. Learn to say no sometimes. Saying no doesn't make you a bad person, it makes you a smart person.

20. Forgive yourself. You know that thing you did once (or maybe a few times) that made you feel bad, embarrassed or ashamed? It's time to let that go. You can't change the things you have done in the past, but you can control your future. Look at it as a learning experience and believe in your ability to change.

CONCLUSION

I Am Back. Life Goes On.

> **"When we are no longer able to change a situation, we are challenged to change ourselves."**
> – Dr. Viktor Frankl, Man's Search for Meaning

> **"If you want to go fast, go alone, if you want to go further go together."**
> – African proverb

"I Am Back"

These are the words that beamed on my phone screen to greet me in the early morning of Father's Day, June 2021. No, they are not the words of my father. His body has transformed from this world to a higher place and his spirit lives on. His picture stands on my desk as I write the final words of this chapter. No, the words are not his. These words are those of a business partner who has become a dear friend to me, whom I helped navigate the journey when he was going through a dark period in his life. We have been working together tirelessly and intensely in the last weeks and months. I have decided to call him Jim here.

Jim, I know you are reading this page with pride and a beaming smile on your face. For privacy reasons I have decided not to disclose your real name although you didn't have any objections. As I write the last words of this chapter in the early hours of the morning, in the solitude of my writing space in my room, it dawns on me even more that the events that transpired after the passing away of my father have been gifts and blessings in disguise. My father is not here anymore to see the enormous transformation I have undergone. Papa, I hope you approve. As part of going through my own dark phases I kept a journal. At the time, little did I know that I would be using these notes about a dark and stormy period in my life to write book! In writing this book I went through the notes of my journal which form the basis of this book. I have used the techniques and insights shared in this book for myself, friends, family and my patients in varying degrees. I don't think most people realise how much strength it takes to pull yourself out of dark place mentally. If you have come this far reading, thank you and well done. It's not that easy holding and reading a book which triggers elements of the dark periods you yourself may have experienced. I commend you. If you have pulled yourself from a dark place mentally, today or any other day, I can only hold admiration for you. If you are still struggling through this battle, feel reassured that you too can put this dark period you are going through behind you.

Oh yes, you can. Yes you can.

I have seen hundreds of patients, friends and family do it and reclaim their lives to make it the masterpiece it was supposed to be in the first place. It is also true that I have seen many patients and friends fall victim to the lies which depression tells. In his book, I Can See Clearly Now, Wayne Dyer, one of my teachers recalls one of the conversation he had with Holocaust survivor and author of the classic Man's Search For Meaning, by Dr Viktor Frankl. In that conversation about the search for meaning, the Holocaust survivor proclaimed, "When we are no longer able to change a situation, we are challenged to change ourselves." I have come to adopt this attitude too. When I was not able to change my situation, I was challenged to change my self. Initially, my business partner, Jim was unable to change his situation, so he was challenged to change himself, and this is what he did.

During a conversation with a friend the other day who is going through dark periods in her life, I urged her to write down and keep notes of what she is going through right now. One day her journey of depression journal will be somebody else's survival guide. I kept notes. I never intended to write a book someday about depression. But, here I am in the solitude of my room, wrapping up a book which I never ever thought would be written. My mentor's words haunted me for quite some time, "If you don't share your experience so somebody out there may be better off, you are selfish." Sheepishly, I began sharing my experience with anybody who would listen. I shared my own story with patients and social media platforms. Here is a sample of a few of the reactions I received.

Hi Ikhenemoh

Thank you for your inspiring videos on Facebook. Currently I have been at home for almost 4 weeks with depression, ups and downs. By listening to your videos, I keep getting a little further and I also start to feel better. The right words, thanks for this! Jolanda

And this rather lengthy one, which still tears me up:

Thank you Ikhenemoh for your insights that made me think. Actually, I have an optimistic nature, yet I found out that I have a lot of underlying pain. Always pushed away. By thinking deeply about a lot of suffering in recent years, a lot of pain has surfaced again. I was shocked to notice that some quotes you share suddenly threw me 20 years back. Much grief for my youngest son's abuse returned. Then I could NEVER cry and just one comment or statement ended up in a valley of tears. Being able to discuss with my son, now 20 years later, that I had to be strong then and take care of the situation on my own. Later a quote related to the loss of a partner. First the divorce of the father of my children, later the sudden death of a new friend, again the need to stay afloat as a strong point came to the fore. Now I have tried to embrace that grief and take time to survey everything. Writing down the situations then, now provides insight where I did not take time for real grief and sorrow. My eldest daughter suddenly left our house, through arguments, and I NEVER got, or really took, the chance to discuss this, was not strong in this situation to oversee it. Now I am trying to re-establish contact. But will have to take the situation as my daughter wishes. There I will have to learn to take my rest, resignation. Depression becomes an obstacle to rational decisions. Clear thinking. Indeed, in order to face the situations one by one, patterns become clear. Thank you Ikhenemoh!

And another:

Mourn my mother, much worse than I expected... I don't put it away anymore, and when the tears come, I let them flow freely. The huge difference now is the nice partner with whom I live, live, talk, celebrate and share. Talking to your love about old pain and listening appears to provide so much insight about the monster called depression. Indeed it makes a big difference if you have people around you who love you and don't want anything from you. Thank you so much for all your insights and your live, dear, videos. It helps me on my way, I am not there yet and I will have to take life as it comes, but I am increasingly able to steer it myself. Love, Marion

And from a young mother with two young kids struggling with depression:

Because of you Dr Ikhenemoh, you gave me hope, clarity and inspiration. I can never thank you enough. Because of you I was able to survive, thank you. Thank you. Thank you.

And this one:

There is something I would like to share with you. Your message helped me so much. Something happened in my life the other day. We have been expecting this for over a decade as my dad suffered severe ill health and is finally out of pain. He passed on Thursday morning. I wanted to share with you so you know how much you have helped me today. Thank you from the bottom of my heart.

I think you have helped so many people with your words coming from your experience and from the heart. You will continue to help so many people deal with grief and forgiveness.– Jessica

My dear reader, if you are riding a storm and still wondering if you will overcome this battle, I say this to you:

"… once the storm is over, you won't remember how you made it through, how you managed to survive. You won't even be sure, whether the storm is really over. But one thing is certain. When you come out of the storm, you won't be the same person who walked in. That's what this storm's all about." – Haruki Murakami, Kafka on the Shore.

It is true that you will have to take some action. Action brings motivation. Motivation brings more action. Whatever you do, please do yourself and me a favour. Before you diagnose yourself with depression, or low self-esteem, make sure you are not surrounded by a bunch of assholes.

When I look back at my life until this moment, there are moments that still blow me away. I have lived in different countries, I have travelled far and wide. I have met the most amazing teachers and scholars. I have loved and lost. I have roamed and slept on the streets of Amsterdam. However, my most transformative moment was my journey with depression. Depression is a label given by our modern society. Whoever called it depression? A "deep resting" would perhaps have been a more appropriate name, or "resting deeply". The writer and poet, Melissa Broder, said it better in her popular Tweet… "What idiot called it "depression" and not there are bats living in my chest and they take up a lot of room. Ps: I always see a shadow."

Call it, or label it, as you wish. Some people still find it distressing to call it depression. A client of mine calls it 'Freddy'. Whenever she notices the early signs rearing their ugly head, she says, 'Freddy is on it again'. This helps her to go through the initial anxiety and worries which she associates with depression. I asked her how she was the other day, and she deadpanned, "Freddy doesn't bother me these days because he doesn't like the name that I gave to him".

The more you research the more you realise that depression is characterised by what we don't know The path to recovery is not one size fits all, especially for a journey which is still full of mystery.

Depression is a hidden disease, it can rear its ugly head at unexpected times. It is normal to experience times of feeling miserable, in a low mood and feeling sad about life. When depression told me its lies I was at the brink of paying the utmost undisclosed price. My mission in writing this book is to never let you come that far, nor to be a victim of those lies. You don't have to fall that far. Help and support is around the corner.

I have also come to learn that suicide is a permanent solution to a temporary problem. My goal is to help you, and your loved ones, overcome depression, guiding you through the journey of healing with concrete action steps and principles which I have outlined in this book. Yes, it is possible to climb out of depression, reclaim your life and make it a masterpiece. Yes, you are a diamond. Yes, you are a masterpiece. Your life is a masterpiece. Never let depression, or any illness, define who you are. You're stronger than you think, braver than you believe and smarter than you know. Depression is a battle that can be won.

After being through this journey, which I would call the most transformative period in my life, I now know that it is an illness that can be most catalytic for positive transformation. I can see clearly now that that night on the highway was a turning point in my life. Aligned with the tools and knowledge of experience, I am able to manage this process of depression when it rears its head. With the skills which I have developed as a survivor and as a doctor, I can take on the lies that depression tells me. I have successfully helped hundreds of patients and their loved ones overcome depression and reclaim their lives but it wasn't always this way.

There is nothing special about me. I have been homeless and experienced depression myself, which has led me to dedicate my life to helping and treating you and your loved ones. You can reclaim your life and make it a masterpiece. Yes, you can, it is going to be a masterpiece, the masterpiece it was supposed to be. Together we can make it happen.

I wish from the depths of my heart that soon, you too can say these words that greeted me on my phone screen on Father's Day in June 2021–I am back!

Sincerely yours,

Dr. Ikhenemoh

ACKNOWLEDGEMENTS

Firstly, I want to thank my uncle, Chief Samson Azebeokhai, for going out of your way to provide shelter for me to live at your home.

Also, Madam Azebeokhai, you believed and saw in me what I couldn't. Thank you for the idea of going to Moscow and Uncle Law, I am forever indebted to you for the role you played in making this book a reality.

Jessen James, where do I start? You have this ability to look past the present. God bless the day I met you and you took me under your wing. For trusting your intuition. You listened attentively and you saw in me what I couldn't. Extra special thanks to Jessen who came up with the idea and title for this book in our first mentorship while we were brainstorming. Simply, brilliant!

To Henk and Ana, thank you for providing for me, literally taking me off the streets and for providing a shelter. You told me that you did not want to see talent wasted. You took care of me selflessly. My first acquaintance with Dutch society started with you.

Anne Sedee – At my most vulnerable moment you showed me love and kindness.

Genia – You have always been supportive, the wings on my back. Amongst all the wrongs I have done, I must have done something right to have you in my life. I hope you approve and this has all been worth it.

Anatol Kuschpeta, thank you for introducing me into the world of personal development, despite my long and initial scepticism.

Cluppie Trouw Rob and Nadia, for being two of the finest friends I could ever have hoped for and for this special club we belong to. Cluppie Trouw Forever.

Shawn, thank you for your continued support. You tick all the boxes of what a best friend is.

Hendrik Vrolijk, thank you for your guidance and help with my first baby steps introducing me into the world of mental health medicine.

To my patients, each and every one of you. Thank you for all the lessons that you taught me. Lessons of resilience, humility, and gratitude to be able to serve you. You have taught me so much more than I have taught you.

Special thanks to my business partners, friends and beta readers who encouraged me, gave me feedback or influenced me in the process of writing this book: Nikita Heller, Kulwinder Kaur, Riya Chaudhury, Henna Penna, Ousha Demello, Chloë Bisson and all members of Facebook Practice Your Live family, my Spanish team Esther Diaz Fernandez, Soraya Salomon Martin, Maria Jose Hurtado, and Facebook group Billion Lives Changed community founded by Jessen James.

My social media team – Cedric Moulin, you and your team helped me find my voice on social media.

Many thanks to Michelle Watson, my book mentor and publisher for your patience, guidance and wisdom.

Sarah Antoniou, my editor who did a great job editing.

My siblings, I didn't choose to be the head of the family as first born, it is the place I find myself now. You have challenged me to rise be up to the occasion and supported me with your love, kindness and support. Nature made us siblings, we made a choice to be friends. Thank you Goddy, Anthonia, Harry, Kate (Mummy), Isaac, Jacob, Kelvin and Augustine.

And to my boy, Okhai, the best decision I have made in my life is the decision not to take my own life. You were and still are my lifeline. Every day is a gift, watching you grow, spread your wings, create and manifest your dreams

REFERENCES AND SOURCES

www.mentalhealth.org.uk

World Health Organization

www.who.int mental health/management/ depression

Mind, www.mind.org.uk   Tel: 0300 123 3393

Black Dog Institute

Haig M, 2015, Reasons to Stay Alive, Edinburg, GB, Canongate books

Maslow A H, 2015. A Theory of Human Motivation. United States of America: Wilder Publications

Dr Wayne W Dyer 2014, I Can See Clearly Now, Hay House Inc

National Suicide Prevention Hotline (US) – 1-800 273 8255

Suicide prevention Netherlands | 113 Zelfmoordpreventie 0800-0113

https://findahelpline.com/i/iasp

Suicide Prevention Hotline (UK) – 08457 909090

Better Help – www.betterhelp.com

Mental Health America – www.mentalhealthamerica.net

ABOUT THE AUTHOR

Dr Francis Ikhenemoh is a speaker, practising family medicine doctor, depression survivor, author and founder of the 'Happiness Doctor.' Born in Africa, he left home at the age of 17 to study in Russia, and then moved to live in Holland, where he roamed the streets of Amsterdam, but pushed beyond all the challenges faced and rode the waves to graduating as a medical doctor.

Dr Ikhenemoh is multilingual and speaks English, Russian and Dutch and he was nominated 'best newcomer' by the Business and Marketing Academy as an individual who devotes his life to sharing tips and strategies that he has learnt through his journey and experience with depression, which he combines with his profession as a medical doctor, to help patients that are living with depression to stop 'existing and start living again. 'He is a man on a mission and deeply passionate about spreading his knowledge and wisdom on various podiums to heal emotional pain, helping not only those battling with depression, but also their loved ones, to overcome and heal their emotional pain.

Award winning speaker "Male Speaker of the Year" and nominee "Best Story Award" of the year.

Made in the USA
Las Vegas, NV
24 February 2022